I'm a Type A
How the Heck Will I Ever
RETIRE?

I'm a Type A

How the Heck Will I Ever RETIRE?

HOW EVEN THE MOST ENERGETIC TYPE A
PERSONALITIES CAN FULLY ENJOY RETIREMENT

TIMOTHY MCINTYRE

I'm a Type A–How the Heck Will I Ever Retire?

Copyright © 2013 Timothy McIntyre.

Cover and Interior Design: Indigo Design, Inc.

bookcoverdesignbyindigo.com

ISBN 978-0-9897492-0-6

Printed in the U.S.A.

To Mom, Dad, and Danny:

I miss you every day.

ACKNOWLEDGMENTS

I am grateful to many people who have helped shape this book with their useful experiences and insightful comments, but especially Bob Bollinger, Chris Lampione, Mark Christoforo, Julanne Sapronetti, Kurt and Sharon Marrin, Susan Boyd, and Joan Francis. The support I received from all of my family and friends throughout this process was phenomenal.

Many of the concepts shared in this book were influenced by discussions I've had with Dr. James N. Watzke, Mary Kunz, Mary Fisk, Karen Butler-Cook, and Dr. Thomas F. Lelio. Thank you so much for your excellent insights into human behavior, and especially into my often dysfunctional behavior!

I was fortunate to have chosen a tremendously talented and dedicated editor, Sarah Aschenbach, without whom this book would not have been possible. Thank you, Sarah, you are a true professional.

I am also indebted to the creative force behind the book's design and messaging, Audria Wooster, who served as designer and marketer-in-chief. Working on creative issues with a logic-minded Type A like me can be both frustrating and daunting, but Audria handled it with class and ease. Audria, you're the best.

I want to thank Ashley Marrin, who is the bright, energetic and gifted coordinator of my social media campaign. Ashley, your future is so bright you'll have to wear shades!

Last, I am forever indebted to my wife, Elaine, not only for her support throughout the development of this book, but for her love and kindness for the thirty years we have been together. She is absolutely right (as she always is) when she says the book that really needs to be written—by someone like her—is how to *live with* a Type A during retirement!

CONTENTS

PROLOGUE

The chair I am sitting on in the therapist's office is adequate, but I notice that his couch looks much more comfortable. No, I decide, I'll just stay where I am. The chair will give me a better angle of view on the therapist so that I'll be more focused on him. I'm hoping he can provide some direct answers for me, and no BS. He has a couple of degrees, so he should know what he's talking about, right? I have an MBA and a slew of professional certifications, and I certainly know my fields of accounting and finance inside-out.

Before he enters the room, I have a couple of minutes to think about my life. I have an excellent job as a manager in a Fortune 500 company, with a good salary. My wife and kids are great; I couldn't ask for a better family. I am physically healthy, probably in the best shape of my life due to intense, daily exercise.

I should be *perfectly* happy.

So, why am I so anxious all the time? Why do I get these strange, panicky feelings that make me so uncomfortable at the most unusual moments? I feel constantly nervous.

It can't be anything serious because, otherwise, I feel great, and things are going so well. My recent promotion to manager of a large financial department at age thirty-two was a big one, but I can handle that. Hell, I can handle *anything* if I just put my mind to it. I always have.

The therapist finally finds his way to the room. He's five minutes late, which is a little annoying, but no big deal if he can deliver the goods. Let's get this over with and get back on track with life!

He appears to be about my age and, in his dowdy, comfortable clothes and horn-rimmed glasses, he looks like a psychiatrist. He asks about my background, interests, and reasons for seeking therapy. He is asking good questions, which is impressive. Yeah, this guy seems sharp. This is going to work.

Then, to my dismay, he starts down an unusual and totally unexpected path of questioning. Every time I relate something I have done or experienced in my life, he asks me how I *felt* at that moment.

"And how did that make you *feel*?" he asks. "What were you *feeling* at the time?"

I tried to be patient and maintain my composure. I really did.

It struck me as a scene from some sitcom about the clueless psychiatrist, you know, the guy who has all the academic training but no idea what real life is all about. What was I *feeling* at the time? What possible difference could that make? To me, it's like asking, "What time was it in China, local time, when that event occurred?" What's the possible relevance? I actually have a huge number of important things I need to *do* every day, okay, and I have absolutely no interest in how I feel about any of them!

He continues on and on like this for the rest of the session: blah, blah, blah, stuck like a broken record on the same silly question. What, did this guy just come back from a seminar or something, armed with this new thing where he keeps asking his clients how they feel about stuff?

What a huge disappointment. And what a friggin' idiot this guy is. I'll come back to see him for another session about the time when hell freezes over...

HOW AND WHY I RETIRED

> " All our dreams can come true, if we have the courage to pursue them. "
>
> —Walt Disney

WORK, WORK, AND MORE WORK

Luck? I don't know anything about luck. I've never banked on it and I'm afraid of people who do. Luck to me is something else: hard work and realizing what is opportunity and what isn't.

—Lucille Ball

I was thirty-nine years old and bored in my job. It was a good job, with the fancy title of Director of Financial Planning and Investor Relations, and I was well paid. The steel company I worked for was large and profitable. And yet, I was not content.

Throughout my career, I usually got restless once I had been in a position for even a year or so. Whenever I started a new position, I threw myself into it with great enthusiasm. I loved to learn and tackle a new challenge. After the learning curve flattened, which happened quickly because I am a fast learner, I would get bored, already looking forward to the next new thing. Before making noise about wanting to move on, however, I always made sure that I made solid contributions to whatever department I was in, both for the benefit of the company and to make my bosses happy.

Early in my career, I mostly worked for very large Fortune 500 companies, where opportunities for strong performers like me to transfer to different departments was often available, and I regularly took advantage of this.

As it turned out, this trait of rarely being satisfied or content and continually hungry for new challenges served me well. I gained a tremendous amount of finance knowledge and leadership experience over the first fifteen years or so of my career. I had worked in almost every possible corporate finance department: financial accounting, cost accounting, auditing, budgeting & forecasting, taxes, cash & investments, mergers & acquisitions, stock & bond financings, financial planning & analysis, and investor relations.

> " This trait of rarely being satisfied or content and continually hungry for new challenges served me well. "

When I worked in an area, I was determined to become an expert at it. As an example, when I was named manager of cash and investments, I found I could get a useful certification, certified cash manager, so I studied for and took the exam. I guess I must have studied pretty hard, because I received the highest score of all two thousand or so test takers. As a result, my wife and I were invited to attend the annual Treasury Management Association conference, all expenses paid, so that I could accept the "Top Scorer Award" and make a presentation to the entire conference. Nice!

I was always clamoring for greater responsibilities, more people to manage, and more money through promotions. I loved to prove myself by taking on bigger and increasingly more difficult challenges. Once when a CEO asked me if I wanted to take responsibility for a new department he was forming in addition to my already heavy responsibilities, all I said was, "Bring it on!"

Therefore, when I decided at age thirty-nine to start looking for a new job with a different company, I had an exceptionally strong resume, stronger than I realized at the time. For some reason, I had never really expected to reach the level of senior officer at a company (the so-called C-level positions, like CFO and CEO). Always during my career, I had kept my head down and worked extremely hard. I did this because I liked to learn, to work hard, and to prove myself. It's not as if I really expected very much out of it or even thought that highly of myself. I suppose, in hindsight, that this unintentional modesty made me an even more attractive candidate for a senior-level position.

I applied for several positions, hoping to find something interesting and challenging, and I landed my first senior-level position, chief financial officer, with a large local software company. I was surprised, but I figured I'd make it work. I was looking for a big, new challenge—well, be careful what you wish for!

It was a huge step forward for me career-wise. I was responsible for the entire accounting and finance function and was a member of the senior management team. I even had a corner office with my own bathroom. This was rarified air for the Irish kid who grew up on the south side of Chicago.

Applied Systems was and is a great company, and I thrived there. The company develops and services software for the insurance industry, mostly insurance agencies. At the time, it had about ten thousand customers and one thousand employees. The owner, Bob Eustace, is a brilliant entrepreneur, if a bit eccentric. (Aren't all great entrepreneurs at least a bit odd?) His son and daughter, Glen and Dawn, who were active in the business, were very bright and helped me adjust to my new position and broad responsibilities.

I must have impressed the owners, because within a year, the family promoted me to president and chief operating officer, putting me in charge of the entire company.

As is my wont, I just put my head down, dug in, and got right to work in my new position. This simple strategy had always served me well, so why not now?

OUT INTO THE WILD BLUE YONDER

You have to be unique and different, and shine in your own way.

—Lady Gaga

Bob Eustace, the owner of Applied Systems, had wanted to sell the company for many years. In fact, I was hired as CFO to coordinate an IPO, which is an initial public offering of stock. An IPO is a way of selling part of the company to outside investors. In my first year at Applied, we attempted an IPO but were unable to complete it because the stock market dipped sharply just as we were ready to market our fledgling stock. The dip would have made it impossible to get Bob's asking price.

All along, Bob was demanding that he obtain a specific price for his company. There was no discussion of seeking a lower price, unless you didn't like your job. You can't blame him. He had started the company from scratch in his garage approximately twenty-five years earlier, and it was a very impressive company.

Considering Applied's earnings at the time I arrived, Bob's minimum price was unrealistically high (surprise!). After I came on board, I learned that, a year or so earlier, a large technology company had taken a look at Applied and offered to purchase the company for less than half of Bob's target value. That had been a complete non-starter.

After the IPO was shelved and when I was made president, I believed that Applied had the potential to be worth Bob's asking price and possibly even much more, albeit with some hard work. Fundamentally, it was a sound company: good products, a strong brand, and loyal customers. While dysfunctional at times, the senior leadership team at Applied had a good mix of talents. The chairman was excellent at sales and had a strong background in technology. I was good at finance and operations and had a knack for business strategy. Bob Eustace was a brilliant businessman with an excellent intuition for what our customers' needs and wants were. Dawn Eustace, his daughter, was very bright and meticulous and could have helped a lot, but, unfortunately, she stepped away from the business to pursue other interests shortly after I arrived. Glen Eustace, Bob's son, was still very involved with the company, and he was a brilliant and gifted finance guy. He also had the highly useful and much appreciated ability to help us "manage" his often-mercurial father so that we were able to keep new programs on track to completion. Our senior team was solid.

Applied had a lot of potential, and I was psyched up to see what we could accomplish.

During my first four years as president, the team and I were highly successful in our efforts. Sales at the company grew steadily and earnings increased dramatically. I had led several initiatives to cut costs and make us more efficient, which, along with many other strategic improvements implemented by our senior team, greatly strengthened the company. We were on a roll.

In 2003, I went into Bob's office and told him I thought we were now in an excellent position to sell the company and meet his asking price. He gave us the green light to hire investment bankers and begin formally marketing the company.

After a long and arduous sales process that lasted about a year, we finally sold the company. But better than that, we had obtained a price that was nearly double Bob's target! It was a huge win for everyone at Applied and a very satisfying accomplishment for the senior team.

Bob, an extremely generous person, took good care of me financially, as well as the rest of the executive group and several other long-term employees. I owned some Applied stock, which Bob had given me when I was named president and which I was able to sell as part of the larger sale of the company. Bob also gave me a very generous additional bonus for my help in selling his company. Not surprisingly, the new owners wanted to install their own hand-picked management team, so I was let go, but not without the benefit of a "golden parachute." I was out of a job, but I was very well set financially.

I was also completely exhausted.

Being president of a large company is difficult enough, but managing the sale of the company along with my day-to-day responsibilities had taken its toll on me. At some point during the year we spent marketing the company, I began to realize that I didn't like my job much. I was good at it, possibly even excellent, but I became less and less happy as time went on.

Looking back now, I think my unhappiness was due to a combination of things. First, I did not want so much people contact. I liked people, but I also enjoyed analysis and project work, which is more solitary. The president's job requires someone very people-oriented and, quite honestly, I found it emotionally draining. I understand that some people are natural "people" people, and they *gain* energy when they interact and spend time with others. Some of us are not, and being around people tends to *drain* us of energy. I think I am the latter.

Also, the one thing I really disliked about corporate life was the lack of time off. A couple of weeks of vacation per year and only a few holidays are standard. And when you are a senior manager, it is difficult to use even the little vacation time you have due to the pressing responsibilities of the job. I lamented not having broader stretches of time off to pursue interests and hobbies and just plain relax.

> " I lamented not having broader stretches of time off to pursue interests and hobbies and just plain relax. "

When I was let go from Applied, I threw myself headlong into the search for another executive position in spite of these misgivings. I had enough money to retire comfortably, but at the time, I thought I'd help run one more company and then maybe call it a career. It seemed like a sensible approach.

In retrospect, I think I was nervous about the prospect of full-time retirement, as most Type As are, but I didn't have any good options for working part-time or scaling back my career. C-level positions are never part-time, and I wasn't interested in consulting or teaching, as many executives are. In a way, I was a bit trapped by my success.

After about six months of searching, I found an excellent position as chief operating officer of a well-established software company in the area. I got a nice haircut, shined my shoes, put on my suit, and toddled off to my first day of work. I felt confident, although not very enthusiastic, about my new position.

I met with the chairman and some other members of the senior team that first morning. They all seemed nice and earnest enough. Still, I had a weird feeling of being just a bit out of place.

I went to lunch by myself, just to think for a little while. Nice company, good people, a decent job, I thought. And then, all of a sudden, it struck me:

Why am I doing this? What's the point?

I didn't want to go back to the office. I didn't want this job. I tried to summon up reasons why I should still want to work.

For the challenge? No, I had finally become weary of all the challenges, at least those presented by the business world. I had never envisioned making it all the way to the position of president, and I was finally satisfied with that accomplishment.

For the money? No, material things were never that important to me. What was I going to buy with the additional money: a bigger house, more-expensive cars, *a boat*? No, thanks. I even thought about taking the job as a service to society. No. I could serve society, and God, as well or better in other ways. Let someone else more motivated and desirous of the job be chief operating officer of this nice company.

I couldn't come up with any good reasons to go back to work that afternoon.

Instead, I went back to the office and told the chairman that, thank you, but I was no longer interested in the position. I said he had a fine company with a great future, but that I wouldn't be able to give him my best, which is what he and his company deserved. He was shocked that I had not even spent a full day on the job, but he had no choice but to let me go.

I had done it. I had cut the cord. The security blanket that was my career was over. I had finally, and likely irreversibly, stepped into that wild blue yonder known as retirement.

I was not entirely sure what this new phase in my life would offer, but I was curious and excited to find out.

THE RETIREMENT DILEMMA
FOR TYPE A PERSONALITIES

 Life is a moderately good play with a badly written third act.

—Truman Capote

ARE YOU ANXIOUS ABOUT RETIREMENT?

Boredom is...a vital problem for the moralist, since half the sins of mankind are caused by the fear of it.

—Bertrand Russell

It was a glorious, typically sunny day in southwest Florida in February. There aren't many parts of the country where you can enjoy an 85-degree day in the middle of winter. I felt very fortunate, lucky to be in Florida on that fine day, and especially lucky to be retired there at the age of forty-six.

Impulsively, I decided to go and play eighteen holes of golf. I had nothing pressing to do and I enjoy the game, so off I went.

At the course, I was paired with three other golfers to make a standard foursome. After we had completed a couple of holes and were waiting on one of the tee boxes for the group in front of us to get far enough ahead that we could hit our drives, I struck up a conversation with one of my golf partners. He was fit and well dressed and appeared to be in his early sixties.

"Do you still work, or are you retired?" I asked. Yes, he still worked. He owned a successful insurance brokerage company that he had started thirty years before in his home state of Ohio. Since I had worked in the insurance software industry for several years, I asked if he knew various people, and we discovered we had a couple of mutual acquaintances. We chatted some more, and I told him how impressive his company was, having been built from scratch.

Later on in the round, out of curiosity, I said, "So, if I might ask, when do you plan to retire?"

He gave me a somewhat nervous look and said, "Oh, I don't know if I'm ever going to retire."

I was intrigued by this unexpected response. "You must really enjoy what you do."

"No. I used to, but not anymore. It's become routine. I don't hate it, but I don't really enjoy it."

"Do you need the money?" I asked. "It sounds like you are pretty well off financially."

"Oh, I'm very well set financially. My business has been successful, and I'm sure I could sell it for a significant amount of money."

Well, I just had to ask the question: "I guess I don't understand; why don't you just pack it in and retire?"

"To be honest," he said, "I don't know if I can retire. I have worked my entire life, often ten hours a day and on weekends, as well. It's all I have ever known. I have no idea what I would do in retirement."

"Don't you have any hobbies or interests? You seem to enjoy golf."

"Not really. I've devoted myself to my career for years. It's what I do. I'll be honest: I'm nervous about how I would spend all that extra time if I retired. What would I do all day?" He sounded a bit exasperated. It was obvious that he had given the idea a great deal of thought—and worry—over the years and was genuinely afraid.

This is a story I have heard repeatedly during my retirement years. It comes mostly from moderate to hard-core Type As, who are usually extremely accomplished and successful and seemingly confident in all aspects of their lives. And yet, they are *afraid* of retirement. Who would have thought it? Not all are as paralyzed by their fears as my golfing partner was, mind you. Many express only a vague sense of uneasiness because they just don't know how they are going to handle being retired. What seems to scare them most is the prospect of so much unscheduled time, or what I like to call "open time." Type As are very structured and productive, and they think of retirement as being defined by a *lack* of structure and productivity. Quintessential "control freaks," Type As are always anticipating and planning; therefore, the prospect of an unstructured future phase of their lives makes them particularly uneasy.

> "What seems to scare Type As most is the prospect of so much unscheduled time, or what I like to call 'open time.'"

I can sympathize. As I got deeper into my career, I became quite anxious about retirement. I felt very uncomfortable with the whole concept. I was typical for a Type A in my general inability to ever really relax. Often when I attempted to relax, I would compulsively jump up and start doing something, whatever popped into my head as needing to be done at that moment. It didn't have to be particularly important. I just wanted to be doing something, *anything,* all of the time.

After I retired, I struggled to deal with all of the open time. I struggled mightily. Bear in mind that I retired at the age of forty-six, so I had a lot of energy and what likely would be decades of time to fill. I cycled between being mind-numbingly bored and frenetically busy with some new project I had dreamed up. Clearly, I was not comfortable in my new existence.

Since then, I have learned a tremendous amount about being a retired Type A. I have sought out and interviewed scores of Type As about the issue of retirement, from those who have decades before they can ever hope to retire to those who have been retired for decades. I have personally tried many different methods and approaches to the problem/opportunity of Type A retirement over my nine years of retirement. Some have worked, and some have failed miserably. Ultimately, because of these efforts and a lot of thought and analysis, I have developed many concepts that have proved to be significant and valuable to Type A retirees. And now, I am ready to share these concepts with you.

THE TYPE A PERSONALITY: WHAT IS IT?

The unexamined life is not worth living.

—Socrates

So, what exactly is the Type A personality? Let's define our terms, shall we?

The Type A and Type B personality theory originally was published in the 1950s. The theory describes two common, contrasting personality types: the high-strung Type A and the easygoing Type B. Part of the original theory is that these patterns of behavior could affect a person's chances of developing coronary heart disease, but there has been much dispute over the years about this possible correlation. Therefore, the connection between personality types and heart disease is not the subject of this book and will not be addressed.

The Type A individual is described as ambitious, aggressive, businesslike, controlling, highly competitive, preoccupied with status, time-conscious, impatient, arrogant, and tightly wound. People with Type A personalities are often high achieving "workaholics" who multitask, push themselves with deadlines, and dislike both delays and ambivalence. Type As generally take little time for self-reflection and find it difficult to relax.

Does any of that sound familiar? For me, it sure does. It describes me to a T!

In contrast, people with Type B personalities are generally creative, patient, easygoing, have little sense of a time schedule, and lack an overriding sense of urgency. They tend to be sensitive to other people's feelings, self-reflective, and find it easy to relax.

Think of extreme Type As and Type Bs as polar opposites

You might have noticed that, when comparing the traits of Type A and Type B personalities, the theory describes each personality as the perfect contrast to, or complete opposite of, the other personality. For each trait, such as patience, Type As and Type Bs are described as polar opposites, with Type As being very impatient and Type Bs exhibiting a high degree of patience. Therefore, for each personality trait addressed by the theory, you can think of the behavior and attitudes of the entire population of humans as running along a continuum such as this:

Personality Trait: Degree of Patience

Extreme Type A	Moderate Type A	Type A/B Mix	Moderate Type B	Extreme Type B
Very Impatient	Impatient	Average Patience	Patient	Very Patient

As you might guess, most people are neither extreme Type As nor extreme Type Bs. Most people have a moderate Type A or Type B personality, or an even mix of traits. However, it also follows that roughly half the people have some or many Type A tendencies, so addressing Type A personality traits, as I do in this book, is relevant to much of the population.

Since we have concluded that extreme Type A and Type B personalities, when compared to one another, are perfect opposites, let's now examine the various traits within each category of Type A and Type B. What is it that correlates all of the traits that constitute a Type A personality or all of the traits that constitute a Type B personality?

Both Type A and Type B personality traits reflect, and arise out of, a certain basic personality. Type As are, at the core, very high-strung and high-energy people. And as a result, they exhibit the related traits of being time-conscious, aggressive, and impatient. These traits are consistent with the Type A's basic high-energy personality. Type Bs are easygoing and relaxed at their core, giving rise to the related traits of patience, little sense of time schedule, lack of urgency, and so on. Therefore, you can see that both Type A and Type B personalities have an internal consistency, as one might expect; hence, the term "personality type."

> " Both Type A and Type B personality traits reflect, and arise out of, a certain basic personality. "

Is it better to be a Type A or a Type B?

The answer is that neither can be described as better or worse or as all good or all bad. For example, is it better to be a driven businessperson who tends to be impatient (Type A) or a gifted professor who has little sense of time schedule (Type B)? Is it better to be impatient or to lack a sense of urgency? I don't think you can definitively say that one is better or worse than the other—just different.

While neither Type As nor Type Bs is intrinsically better or worse than the other, it appears that both have traits that might be considered strengths and traits that might be classified as weaknesses. Type As usually multitask well, but then they are impatient with their fellow workers. Type Bs tend toward creativity, and in the process they might miss a deadline or two.

I have observed that most strengths—or desirable personality traits—have some corresponding disadvantage or less desirable tendency, similar to the flip side of a coin. You might be a very industrious person, which is generally considered desirable, but at the same time, you are probably also somewhat more arrogant and impatient than a lot of your less ambitious peers. Or, if you can fairly be described as relaxed, you also may have the tendency to be less timely or reliable than others.

How much are we able to change?

Do we have the ability to change with regard to these personality traits? Specifically, can we soften the less desirable tendencies? Yes, some of the expression of these traits can be managed, especially if you are willing to work at being self-aware and are open to change. In fact, the entire practice of psychology is essentially predicated on this belief. You may inherently have difficulty relaxing, but you can learn to be somewhat calmer through understanding certain concepts and practicing certain techniques. If you are very time-conscious, you can moderate this trait with self-awareness and practice. You might not be able to always, or even consistently, change your attitudes and behaviors, but change for the better is possible.

Much of this book is based on the belief that people with Type A personality traits can change, or "expand," their personalities to make their lives more enjoyable and satisfying.

Available testing instruments

If you are unsure just how much of a Type A personality you are and would like an objective tool to assess your level of Type A tendencies, several free and easy-to-use questionnaires are available on the Internet. You can go to *www.queendom.com*, search "type a personality test" and take the "Type A Personality Test - Abridged." Also, you can go to *www.pyschologytoday.com,* click on "Tests" and then on "Personality," and take the "Type-A Personality" test. These testing instruments are similar and informative.

> " Accept and embrace that you are a Type A. "

If you are like me, though, you will simply say, "Guilty as charged," and accept and embrace that you are a Type A.

HOW TECHNOLOGY AND MODERN CULTURE REINFORCE TYPE A BEHAVIOR

The system of nature, of which man is a part, tends to be self-balancing, self-adjusting, self-cleansing. Not so with technology.

—E. F. Schumacher

The changes in technology that have occurred in the last thirty years, and especially in the last ten, have had the greatest impact on our culture and our daily lives of any single factor during this time.

How technology is changing human behavior

In fact, technology has seen such rapid and accelerating development in recent years that it appears to be causing corresponding changes in human behavior. Faster and more convenient mobile devices that connect us to the Internet and each other are now ubiquitous. The Internet boom and associated dizzying increase in the use of social media have transformed our daily routines and behaviors.

At first, we had such early technologies as "dumb" phones (not Internet-connected) and PDAs. Now, we have smart phones, tablets, and even mini-tablets. Surely, these devices will continue to evolve, and in turn, we will become increasingly connected. And what do we do with these devices? Well, most of us email, text, tweet, and post almost constantly. A *Newsweek* article revealed that, "the average teen processes an astounding 3,700 texts a month." Yikes!

Increased impatience

Not only are we always connected, but also we get information so readily and quickly that many of us are becoming less patient every day. This phenomenon is reflected in the big technology companies' advertising, their pervasive ads both reflecting trends in our society and helping to reinforce them. TV commercials for smart phones that use the faster 4G technology show twenty-somethings kidding each other about slow receipt of emails or tweets with the less speedy 3G network. "That was *so* twenty-seven seconds ago!" the guy with 4G remarks as his 3G friend *finally* receives an email that was sent to both of them. Twenty-seven seconds ago? Huh?

> " It is considered a sign of weakness to do only one thing at a time. Just ask your boss, right? "

It seems that our society's cultural adaptation to technologies such as mobile devices and social media really are changing our attitudes and behavior, and some of this change appears to be moving in the direction of enhancing and reinforcing Type A behaviors.

As the twenty-somethings' example above illustrates, an increase in impatience appears to be one such shift that is occurring. We can't sit still and wait for anything, anymore. Our heads might explode!

Mandatory multitasking

Also, multitasking has become ubiquitous. It is considered a sign of weakness to do only one thing at a time. Just ask your boss, right? Unfortunately, multitasking can result in a lack of focus on the task of the moment, such as inattention at meetings or while driving as we play with our smart phones or tablets. When it first became pervasive, I thought talking on the phone while driving was crazy, but now people are *texting* while they're driving. How can looking down at your phone or tablet while driving lead to anything but carnage and death?

I realize I'm revealing my advanced age here just a bit, but so be it. However, I must ask: Is it old age or just common sense?

Advances in technology are making us more controlling and time-conscious, which are classic Type A behaviors. We now expect to be in complete control of all aspects of our lives at all times: work, family, social connections, news, sports, and so on. We can't be out of the loop for even a moment or bad things will happen! Time has become our master and keeper because everything must happen immediately. When lack of an immediate response requires us to wait, we get angry and frustrated.

So, is technology turning us all into extreme Type A personalities? Probably not, but it appears to be enhancing and reinforcing some of these behaviors. The same *Newsweek* article I quoted above also observed that: "The research is now making it clear that the Internet is not 'just' another delivery system. It is creating a whole new mental environment, a digital state of nature where the human mind becomes a spinning instrument panel."

Gary Small, a neuroscientist and brain researcher at UCLA, has found that the brains of frequent Internet users are twice as active as those of less frequent users. He believes that this results in a rewiring of the brain. No one yet knows whether the rewiring is permanent.

As I've said before, being a Type A is neither a good thing nor a bad thing. There are positive and negative aspects. It's just interesting to note this recent cultural shift in the direction of Type A behaviors.

Well, at the very least, all of this Type A behavior makes one person happy. If this continues, I'm going to sell a hell of a lot more books!

HOW LONG SHOULD YOU CONTINUE TO WORK?

Ambition and death are alike in that neither is ever satisfied.
—Proverbs 27:20

This Bible quote is one of my favorites, and I quote often from the Bible throughout this book. I want to take this opportunity, however, to recognize that many people are not as spiritual or religious as I am, and that there are many different (and differing) faiths. I respect all believers and non-believers alike. However, I also feel strongly about my spirituality and how it has helped me throughout my life, especially through difficult transitions like my early retirement as a Type A. If one or more of you, due to my convictions, were to decide to reawaken some past spirituality or strengthen your current beliefs, I'll admit I would be pleased. Throughout this book, where my religious beliefs come into play, I express them because they are part of who I am, and this book is meant to be a full and honest portrayal of my experiences as a Type A in retirement and what I believe.

Enough said. On with the issue of when to choose to retire.

Everyone struggles with deciding when to walk away from full-time employment. It is a difficult decision. For most people, it is a permanent decision; there is no turning back. Once you walk away from your employer, and especially if you start taking a pension, it is usually game over. Even if you want to continue your career, as an older person it can be difficult or impossible to find a similar position. Companies love to hire "young and cheap."

If you don't have enough money to retire, then you keep working, of course, either full-time or part-time, because it is a necessity. If you have accumulated enough money to retire (through pensions, Social Security, and savings), and you dislike your job, then the decision is easy: you quit and do what you really want to do every day.

If you like or even love your job, which incredibly some people actually do, when to retire is a tougher decision, regardless of your money situation. I think about it this way: If you were lying on your deathbed, having worked your entire life up to that point, and you began thinking back over your life, would you be disappointed? Would you feel you made a mistake or missed something by not pursuing other passions and aspirations? Some people simply don't have many interests outside of work, and they aren't the types to explore new areas. That's okay. In that case, do what you love for the rest of your life or for as long as you are able and an employer will have you.

I'm going to bet that a lot of you want more out of life than just your career. It's not that your career is completely uninteresting or outright painful, but for many it eventually becomes routine, at best. And by its nature, every career is limiting in terms of opportunities for new knowledge, varied experiences, and continuing challenges. Don't you want some different experiences? Wouldn't you enjoy an opportunity to try things that have always intrigued you, but you never had the time to pursue?

Another way of looking at it is this: One fateful morning before you are about to toddle off to your job for the zillionth time, do you want your spouse to walk into the kitchen only to find you face-down in your cornflakes? Do you want to work your butt off every day of your adult life, head-down and focused on the job, only for it all to end in this ignominious fashion? Wouldn't that be a disappointing result? For me, it would be. And if you agree, then you probably should not work full-time at your chosen career for too long, because it could very well end up being for the rest of your life.

Some people might be able to achieve "the best of both worlds" by scaling back at their current jobs, working part-time, taking on fewer customers, being a consultant, or finding some similar arrangement. If that's the case and you can earn some extra money and still have time to pursue other avenues of your life, then great, you might very well choose to do that. For Type As, this can be an especially good choice, allowing you to ease your way toward full-time retirement while also maintaining some structure and productivity.

> " One fateful morning before you are about to toddle off to your job for the zillionth time, do you want your spouse to walk into the kitchen only to find you face-down in your cornflakes? "

However, most of us will not have that option. Moreover, most people end up being forced to end their careers suddenly, against their wishes and with little or no notice or recourse. This happens because of health problems, corporate downsizings, corporate mergers/acquisitions, layoffs, perceived "performance issues," and the like. And when you leave the workforce as an older worker, as I said, it is usually difficult or impossible to find a similar job.

If you are forced to end your career and you need the money, a new type of work, possibly part-time, could be the ticket. This situation opens up the opportunity to try something new and different, if you can find the right job. Maybe, if you're lucky, you can find something that is even a little fun and not too demanding stress- or time-wise.

I want to explain the Bible quote I chose to start this chapter because it is a bit cryptic, but its message is critically important. I think what is meant by "death is never satisfied" is that death continues to take more and more of us, and its appetite is never sated. It just continues to want more and the wanting will never end or be satisfied. Ambition is like that. You can pursue greater success, status, and riches, but somehow the need for more of the same seems only to grow and strengthen within you rather than come to satisfaction. Ambition is a self-reinforcing cycle that cannot and will never be fully satisfied or attained, and you should recognize it as such.

You will need to make a conscious decision at some point that more ambition and success are not what you want out of life. Maybe, just maybe, what you really seek is less, different, and more enjoyable. Or perhaps it is simply peace and contentment.

Later on, I will explain how to figure out what you really and truly enjoy doing. We will explore this issue in quite a bit of depth since it is so critical to your happiness.

THE TWO-PRONGED RETIREMENT STRATEGY

I still find each day too short for all the thoughts I want to think,
all the walks I want to take, all the books I want to read,
and all the friends I want to see.

—John Burroughs

For Type A personalities like us, I believe the optimal retirement strategy involves applying two seemingly contrasting, but in fact complementary, approaches: first, play to your strengths; then, expand your horizons.

Play to your strengths

This is the first prong of my two-pronged retirement strategy. We Type As have a lot to be proud of. We are highly productive and useful members of society. Man would never have made it to the moon had it not been for Type As like us. In short, we're the ones who get things done. Who's going to do all the work—those procrastinating Type Bs? I'm afraid not.

It simply makes no sense to deny who you are. You are an individual created with certain God-given strengths, and you should utilize them. Ignoring or denying those strengths would be a grave disappointment to the One who made you. Trying to be someone you are not also would be tremendously frustrating and unproductive for you personally.

When I look back on my business career, I see now that one of my many mistakes was spending too much time trying to fix people. Eventually, I realized that it is best to play to their strengths. Place people in jobs that are a good, natural fit for their personalities, and it is likely that they will thrive.

I'll use the current example of Lisbeth Salander, the main character in *The Girl with the Dragon Tattoo*. It would make no sense to put this brilliant and talented researcher, who has an abrasive personality, in charge of the sales department of your company, regardless of how much training and development you plan to give her, right? I'm pretty sure that's right.

So, as a Type A person, you should keep some structure in your life and continue setting and achieving goals when you retire. These are good things. They are who you are, and you will be happier if you are utilizing your God-given strengths.

"Play to your strengths" simply means to surrender to and use your Type A inclinations during retirement.

You might say that there is no need for any instruction, that you already know how to be a Type A because you've been doing it all your life. That's true, but I think I can provide some insights from my experiences that will make you even more productive and satisfied in retirement.

I will present you with a set of detailed, concrete steps, which I refer to as the "4 Ps:" *passions, priorities, purpose,* and *projects*. The 4 Ps provide a specific road map for how to fully engage in retirement as a Type A so that you will spend time on the "right things" and maximize your enjoyment and satisfaction.

Expand yourself

What do I mean by "expand yourself?" I mean expanding your personality to embrace ways of thinking and behaving outside your normal comfort zone, things that do not come so naturally to you as a Type A. Initially, it sounds simple enough. In fact, it is hard to expand yourself. Developing and changing in any way is very difficult, as I'm sure most of you have discovered. It usually starts with some proclamation: "I'm going to be more patient with the kids." That lasts for a day or so, right? Or: "I'm going to relax more," but you go to work the next day and a pile of projects has you staying there until the wee hours. Or: "I'll *never* drink again!" (No need to elaborate on this example!)

And yet, you might ask, and rightfully, "Why should I change?"

The reason it is a good idea to make some effort to change and develop is that even a small amount of personal development will greatly enhance the quality of your life in retirement. No, it isn't easy, nor should you try to completely change who you are. That would be foolish and ultimately unsuccessful.

As Type As, we have a great desire to have it all. We often go at challenges with everything we've got, with every bit of energy in our being. We don't want to leave anything on the table when we're done.

And what is life if not our biggest challenge? Don't we all want to get the full range of experiences available? Yes, most people do. Yet, our personalities tend to limit us in key ways. This is true for everyone's personalities, and not just for Type

As. However, there are things we Type As are very good at, and simply because we are good at them, we tend to be weak in other areas—the "flip side" of the coin.

Embracing change will enable you to live a fuller life in retirement, to experience it in a way that is even more satisfying and enjoyable than your life prior to retirement. A better life is there for the taking, although it requires some effort. Retirement, with its open canvas, is an especially opportune time to cultivate expanded experiences.

> " Retirement, with its open canvas, is an especially opportune time to cultivate expanded experiences. "

Most people would like to be able to truly, fully relax. As a Type A, wouldn't you find this pleasant for a change? What if you could slow down so that you could enjoy the "process" of everything you do, no matter how simple or routine? While it might be a major improvement in satisfaction if you could enjoy all of the complexity and richness of an activity, our first instinct as Type As is to rush through and cut short to get to the next activity. Wouldn't it be nice to enjoy activities that once made you so anxious that you wanted to jump out of your skin, like touring a local museum or zoo for an entire day? Wouldn't it be fun to relax and fully experience just going for a leisurely walk, playing with your pet, or even just savoring your lunch? Wouldn't it be pleasurable to live as fully and as joyfully as you possibly can, enjoying all things, even the simplest of them, with your full attention?

Now, let's explore in detail how you can use your considerable abilities as a Type A to maximize your retirement experience. After all, the retirement phase of our lives is the last of our major challenges, right?

PLAY TO YOUR STRENGTHS

> Always be yourself, express yourself, have faith in yourself, and do not go out and look for a successful personality and duplicate it.
>
> —Bruce Lee

ADD STRUCTURE AND MEANING TO YOUR RETIREMENT: THE "4 Ps"

Man – a being in search of meaning.

—Plato

During my first couple of years in retirement, one thought dominated my consciousness. It was an uncomfortable, worrying thought, and I simply could not shake it.

I just had so much time, so many days, so many hours in a day. Too much time.

My discomfort about having so much time permeated everything I did and was reflected in every aspect of my attitude and behavior. It drained me of energy and enthusiasm, and that was highly unusual for me. I was in a malaise. I kept active, but it was forced busyness. I felt little joy.

Just keeping busy was not enough

When I first retired from Applied Systems after the sale of the company, I soon began searching for a new job. The thought of having a job was a security blanket, I think. At least I knew what work life was like. Once I realized I didn't really want that and fully committed to retirement, I plunged into a period of non-stop motion and busyness. I took golf lessons and went to the driving range every day to practice. Soon, I realized I didn't really like golf very much, and the constant swinging of the club was aggravating an old lower-back injury. I started weightlifting more aggressively, which was fun for a little while, but I didn't find it particularly fulfilling or satisfying. Then, I began a walking program, walking several miles every day all around the local area. This used up some energy and time, but it was not very gratifying, just like the other activities.

> " I was outwardly engaged, but not inwardly. I was tentative, unsure of myself, hesitant about life. What was missing in my life in retirement? "

I was outwardly engaged, but not inwardly. I didn't feel like myself. In fact, I wasn't my usual confident, motivated, and larger-than-life persona. I was tentative, unsure of myself, hesitant about life. And I wasn't happy.

What was missing in my life in retirement? What was causing me so much angst? What was it that I simply could not live without?

Passions, priorities, and purpose: The missing ingredients

I began a search for answers. Why was I feeling this way, and what could I do about it? It was during this period of confusion, searching, and self-analysis that I developed the 4-Ps Process.

The missing ingredients in my life were *passions, priorities,* and *purpose.* Once I had developed these, the *projects* I selected to work on from that point forward gave me real satisfaction and joy and were no longer just "make work" projects.

Applying the 4 Ps was like turning on the lights. I went from being unenthusiastic, wobbly, and melancholy to being energized, focused, and happy. I was totally transformed. The joy was back. The new thought that dominated my thinking was:

There is not nearly enough time—not enough days, and not enough hours in a day, to do everything I want to do!

I want to share the 4-Ps Process I have developed so that you can experience as much joy in retirement as I do.

The first step is determining what your *passions* in life are. What do you truly enjoy and value? Are you passionate about your family? Do you love to care for and immerse yourself in your family and feel that life would be meaningless without it? If you do, then family is one of your passions, maybe your most important. You might find you are passionate about a hobby or interest, a form of exercise or sport, an intellectual pursuit, a charitable cause, or something entirely different. The list is endless and is limited only by your imagination.

Once you have identified some or all of your passions, the next step is to order them in terms of *priority.* For many of you, family may likely be more important than, say, your love of movies or boating or reading. But it may not be the case, and if so, you should be honest with yourself so that you determine your real priorities. To this end, you will find a simple test in the chapter on ordering your priorities to help you determine your true priorities.

Third, you will use what you learn about your passions and priorities to develop a single, stated *purpose* for your life. Hopefully, this purpose will be what gets you flying out of bed in the morning, filled with enthusiasm and excitement for the new day. It will serve as your primary guiding force during retirement.

Last, you will structure *projects,* or detailed goals and activities, around your passions, priorities, and purpose. This is where you turn these ideas into actionable events and activities.

Let's begin this process by identifying your passions so you can jump-start your retirement and begin living as fully as possible.

FIND YOUR PASSIONS

Happiness is mostly a by-product of doing what makes us feel fulfilled.

—Benjamin Spock

Do you just love to play golf? I mean, do you enjoy it so much that you would play it every day if you could? Or do you have a hobby or interest that you love to immerse yourself in, like restoring cars, playing the piano, or painting? Maybe you just adore your spouse, who is your best friend and soul mate, and love to spend every available moment together. Or maybe you relish playing with your grandchildren so much that you completely lose yourself in the joy of the moment.

> " Passions: things that bring you joy, fill your spirit, and put a spring in your step. "

These are all examples of passions: things that bring you joy, fill your spirit, and put a spring in your step. During their working lives, some people have developed more and deeper passions than others. If you don't have any obvious passions yet, don't worry, because I'll show you how to find yours.

To add structure and "bring life" to my discussion of passions, priorities, purpose, and projects, I will use my own experiences in retirement. So far, my journey has been quite interesting and has had many unexpected twists and turns, a lot of setbacks, and the occasional victory. All of these offered useful learning experiences that I'd like to share.

Identify what you love without judging yourself

When I first retired and began thinking about what I truly value and enjoy in life, I was fortunate to have a long list. I'm lucky to have a naturally curious spirit that has led me to develop quite a few interests outside of work. I have observed that we all have a zest for life if we dig down deep enough and give ourselves the license to explore. The most important thing in this phase of identifying your passions is to be open-minded, receptive. Until you start trying things, you won't know for sure what you might really like, or even love.

This was my first stab at listing my passions, in no particular order:

- God
- Elaine (my wife)
- Family (my children and extended family)
- Exercise
- Dogs
- Travel
- Finance

What struck me first was that it was such an odd list. Was I some kind of weirdo? Dogs, exercise, and finance? Should I spend my retirement years teaching yoga and taxes to poodles? If I added sex to my list of passions, I could come up with some even weirder combinations.

Anyway, the idea at this early point is not to be judgmental, so don't worry if you have a wacky list, too. Just consider what you are or could be passionate about without any judgment or editing. It is what it is.

What did you enjoy before work claimed you?

Let's say your easily identified passions are quite limited or even non-existent. I know many people for whom this is the case, and again, it's okay. You've been working your butt off trying to make a living, so you haven't had time to fool around with hobbies, passions, or whatever. That is understandable.

One simple way to uncover passions is to recall what you liked doing as a youth. What did you truly enjoy? Was Little League baseball fun? Did it make you happy to just be with your friends, chatting and being part of a group? Maybe a subject in school intrigued you but you never had a chance to fully explore it, like psychology, philosophy, or world history. Some kids like taking things apart or building things with blocks.

> " One simple way to uncover passions is to recall what you liked doing as a youth. "

The things that intrigued and fascinated you in your formative years are very revealing. This was the time when you let your spirit take its natural course, unrestrained by the expectations of other people and society. You went with the flow and your innermost feelings.

Based on this self-examination, write your list of potential passions. You might be quite convinced about some of them, and others will just be inklings. Again, that's okay. Write down all of the possibilities and keep adding to your list as you think of new things.

Start doing the things on your list

Whether your initial list is long or short, the next step is critical: Begin actively doing the things on your list. I have found that you don't really know for sure if you are passionate about something until you spend time doing it. During this trial-and-error process, strive to quell any fear of failure. What is failure, anyway, in the retirement phase of your life and in the process of identifying passions? Does it even apply? I don't think so. Let's say you try something and it isn't as much fun as you thought it might be. So what? Just move on to the next opportunity on your list.

The trial-and-error process is useful in two ways. First, your list may contain things that you need to try in order to find out if you even really like them. At some point, I had added philosophy and photography to my list of potential passions because both of these intrigued me. After spending some time reading about and experiencing these subjects for a while, I discovered that I actually had little real or deep interest in either, so I moved on. Even though they didn't pan out, it was worthwhile to learn more about them.

Second, you may know you have a passion for something, but you need to figure out how you will participate in it during retirement, and that can take some trial and error. For example, I have a passion for finance, but I needed to figure out how I could best incorporate it into my retirement. I studied finance in college and it was my primary career. Even though I had decided that I no longer wanted to work in the field full-time, I have continued to have an intellectual interest in the subject. There are always new developments occurring in the field, and I wanted to keep abreast of them. I find the subject stimulating and challenging.

Initially, I thought I might want to become a certified financial planner. Certification involves taking five courses over a period of two years or so, which can be done on a self-study basis, and passing a rigorous examination. After becoming certified, I thought I might work in the field, for pay, as a part-time second career.

Accordingly, I enrolled in a CFP program and took a course. However, as I was sitting in the library on one bright and sunny day, slaving away over a textbook on federal taxation and watching people ride by on their bikes, I thought, "Are you nuts?" I had to wonder what I was doing, because it was altogether too much work and effort.

I decided instead to use my already significant finance knowledge on a pro-bono basis to help family members and friends with their investments, college planning, and retirement planning. I would avoid giving advice on areas that I was weak on, like estates and trusts, which are better left to a lawyer, anyway. This would give me a reason to stay current in the key areas of personal finance, and it suited my level of enthusiasm for work, which was moderate to low. Nice!

I have been providing financial planning services to family and friends for several years now, and I really enjoy it. It's just the right balance for me.

I continued to explore my passions. I had an interest in baking, and I thought it might be creative and fun. Besides, I love sugar and desserts. My mom, rest her soul, loved sweets, too, and she was an expert baker. I figured what the heck; let's give it a whirl. Well, I discovered that I really enjoy the whole process of baking. When you can take your time with it, it's relaxing. And I certainly love the finished products! I now have about twenty dessert recipes that I have developed and perfected, and they are quite good.

I also like to read for relaxation as well as for learning, so I tried many different types of books until I discovered that I love to read true-crime books for relaxation and certain types of self-improvement books for learning. Nowadays, I always have one or two books that I am in the process of reading, and these provide a great way to wind down at the end of the day.

As a last example, I recognized that I had an interest in learning how to draw, so I enrolled in a drawing class for adults at a local community college. I expected to be terrible at it; after all, I was an accountant, but I also thought I might enjoy creating a piece of art from scratch. After taking the course and making several drawings, I discovered exactly the opposite: I was very good at it, but I didn't enjoy it. My family and friends were shocked at how accurate my drawings were. They said, "You didn't draw this!" Hah, yes I did! But I didn't enjoy the process. I approached it with such a detailed and almost obsessive mindset that it felt like work. Whenever I thought about spending some time working on a drawing, it felt like homework. No fun. Go figure! I scratched drawing as a hobby off my list because of just plain lack of joy.

Exploring your passions can be interesting, illuminating, frustrating, and thoroughly unpredictable, and retirement is the perfect time for experiences like this! I hope that you will choose to continue searching for and pursuing your passions for the rest of your existence. As you learn more about yourself and continue to explore the world with all its possibilities and complexities, you will continue to uncover new, unexpected, and exciting passions.

Never stop pursuing your dreams lest you wither and die!

ORDER YOUR PRIORITIES

[Turn on] the TV, and you'll be bombarded with suggestions of how to have a successful life. Some of these suggestions are deeply unhelpful to our own projects and priorities—and we should take care.

—Alain de Botton

Once you have identified at least a few things that you are passionate about, it is useful to prioritize them. Prioritizing is a strong suit for Type As, and now we are going to apply it to finding purpose in retirement. Obviously, you will value some of the passions on your list more than others. Prioritizing them will enable you to focus your time in retirement on what is most important to you and make decisions on how you will allocate your time and energy.

Our time on this earth is precious, and it is limited. By the time we retire, we have already spent much of the time we have available. Why not use what we have left doing what we truly love?

How I prioritized my passions

As I looked over my list of passions, choosing my number one priority was easy. I love God and believe in Him completely. He's my guy! Therefore, having faith in God and learning to know and love Him was my highest priority.

Initially, I thought my second priority should be faithful service to God by helping and serving others. I wanted to glorify and honor God with my life.

Then, I realized I was forgetting something, and it was something I had often ignored during my life, and that was the simple but critically important concept of taking care of me. Being such a hardcore Type A had led me to ignore my needs and repeatedly work myself to the bone. While this made me extraordinarily productive, at least for a while, it also inevitably left me tired, anxious, unhappy, and, ultimately, less productive. In this depleted state, I also often lacked sufficient compassion, caring, and kindness when I dealt with others, including family and friends.

> " I love God and believe in Him completely. He's my guy! "

I decided that I was going to stop neglecting myself. In retirement, I was going to properly prioritize, and for once fully embrace, the concept of taking care of me. I did not mean this in a selfish way, mind you, but just as a means of being compassionate toward myself, whom God made, and so I could be happy and productive.

Now, I had identified my top three priorities in retirement:

- God (to love and know Him)
- Taking care of me
- People (to be kind to others and serve them)

Upon further reflection, I was certain that these were my key passions in life. They felt right.

After I had developed my top three priorities, the rest were easy to determine. They were:

- Our home and personal finances
- Exercise (my favorite hobby)
- My social life and hobbies like travel, dogs, baking, reading, etc.

I decided that, while my first three priorities would be permanent and unchanging, I would be more flexible about the others as I changed and as conditions changed. So, my top three priorities would form a solid, concrete foundation, while the others could change according to circumstances.

A simple test for validating your priorities

Let's look at two possible priorities. We'll call them Passion A (family) and Passion B (hunting). Under normal circumstances, Passion A, family, is the higher priority, right? That is certainly what most of us would tell someone if asked. But the real test is what you choose to do when you have a conflict in your schedule. What you decide to do in that circumstance is most telling. Remember, actions speak louder than words!

Let's say you planned to go out of town on a hunting trip with your buddies (Passion B). You greatly enjoy these trips, and you've been looking forward to this one for a while. As luck would have it, your wife's father suddenly becomes gravely ill a couple of days before your trip. You know that your physical presence and emotional support during this difficult time would be of tremendous assistance to your wife and her family (Passion A). What do you do?

Sorry, but if you go on that trip, your real priorities have been determined. I'm not saying that one exception always breaks the rule, but stating that your family is your higher priority becomes a difficult case to make.

You just have to be honest about what your real priorities are. What is the point of trying to kid yourself or fool others? It will only cause you frustration. If you truly love hunting, or traveling, or golf, or just spending time alone more than anything else, don't deny it. This bears repeating: Don't deny who you are. Do what you love. Will there be consequences? Of course. There are always consequences with any course of action. But what's the alternative? The alternative is unhappiness and discontent, which benefits neither you nor those around you.

CHOOSE A SINGLE PURPOSE

The soul which has no fixed purpose in life is lost; to be everywhere, is to be nowhere.

—Michel de Montaigne

Having a single, stated purpose is powerful.

Sure, you could skip this step and simply use your priorities to make decisions about what to do during retirement. Yet having a purpose adds tremendous focus and energy to your life.

Your purpose answers the following critical questions:

- Why am I here?
- How can I best use my unique talents and gifts?
- What does my life stand for?
- When I am gone, what will I have done that really mattered?

Most people will agree that these are important questions. In fact, are any questions more important?

No doubt, you have done worthwhile and rewarding things during your work life. That's great. But now, you're retired, and it's pretty important for you to decide how you will spend the remaining, precious days of your existence. Your purpose provides the answer.

How will you spend your days?

When I first thought about my purpose in retirement, what quickly popped into my mind was that I wanted to glorify God.

For me, that was a very good answer. Above all else, I want to go to heaven when I die. It is the fundamental Christian ideal. Very simply, it captures what I am all about, what motivates me, and what is most central to my being.

> " What was I actually going to *do* each day when I woke up in the morning? I wanted the answer to that. "

As I thought about it more, though, I decided it would be useful to take my purpose one step further by making it more specific. It was an excellent purpose, and right for me, but it was also a little vague. I mean, what was I actually going to *do* each day when I woke up in the morning? I wanted the answer to that.

I looked at my list of priorities. The first was "to know and love God." Was there a more specific purpose I could develop directly from that? I decided not. I thought about it a lot and ultimately determined that I would pursue this priority on a daily and hourly basis as part of my regular life, and not in any more specific fashion. For example, I didn't want to become a minister. It doesn't suit me.

My second priority was to take care of me, and while this would be a high priority, I did not plan to spend most of my time on it. This priority would win out if there was a conflict, such as when I wanted to push myself to accomplish more, but was also tired, frustrated, and depleted. However, I did not expect to spend most of my day focusing on myself.

What of combining my first and third priorities in acts of kindness and service that would honor and glorify God and benefit people?

That was it! That would form the basis for an unambiguous purpose to guide and energize me in retirement for the rest of my existence here on earth.

How to develop your purpose statement

So, after much wrangling and many, many revisions, I developed the following purpose for myself:

To be kind, helpful, and generous to my family,
friends, and others

I chose the words carefully so that my purpose statement would have maximum meaning to me and guide me explicitly as I determined how I would spend my time and effort.

Now, to illustrate how you can work to develop your own purpose statement, I will briefly discuss each piece of my purpose statement. I want to explain why my purpose holds so much meaning for me, and why each word you choose in your purpose is so important. If you take great care in developing this statement for yourself, it has the potential to completely energize you and fully stand the test of time.

The first part of my statement involves *types of actions* I would undertake. They are:

- Kind: Being caring and compassionate in all of my simple, daily interactions with people
- Helpful: Expending *time and effort* to help people
- Generous: Expending *money* on people

These were the ways I would spend my time in retirement! I was excited about a life of service. Also, I had listed the above actions in order of priority. Most important was simply to be a good person as I went through each day. Whether it was with my spouse first thing in the morning, a neighbor I met as I walked my dog, a sales clerk at the mall, or a call from my brother in the evening, I would strive to treat all with whom I came into contact in a kind and compassionate manner. Next most important would be to spend my time helping others. This would be reflected in actions as simple as helping my wife bring in the groceries or assisting a friend who is in need, or as involved as volunteering my time several hours a week or joining a charitable organization in a leadership role. Last, but still important, I would use whatever financial resources I could afford to assist people.

The second part of my purpose involves the *objects of my actions,* or those toward whom my efforts would be directed. Again, I listed these in order of importance to me:

- Family: My spouse, children, and extended family
- Friends: Self-explanatory
- Others: Strangers (Oh, and other of God's creatures, too, like animals)

For a while, I wondered whether it was wise and just to prioritize family and friends over other people in my efforts at service. My family and friends are all comfortable and pretty well off financially, so I thought maybe I should instead help others more, many of whom are in so much more need. It was a close call, but I decided to apply the validation test: if a family member or friend required assistance while I was helping others, and I had to decide whom to help, I would assist the relative or friend. As a former mayor of Chicago once said, if you're not going to take care of your family, then whom are you going to take care of? In good conscience, I couldn't let them down in a time of need. But it was also true that my family and friends would not need help often, which meant I would likely spend more of my days and weeks helping other people. In this way, I would make family and friends a higher priority, but realistically, I would spend more of my available time on others. This made sense to me.

I have been living this purpose for several years in retirement, and I am extremely pleased with it. It has stood the test of time. I find true joy and satisfaction in it. I highly recommend spending however long it takes to develop your unique purpose. It pays a lot of dividends.

While I have chosen service as my purpose in retirement because I find it extremely meaningful, I am not at all suggesting that you should choose this as your purpose. Certainly, service is a laudable goal, but there are many other worthwhile purposes, and you must choose your own path. The whole idea behind the 4-Ps Process is to discover what *you* find energizing and motivating. You may decide that caring for yourself by working on self-healing or self-discovery is your highest purpose at this point in your life. Whatever it is, let no one else judge the value of *your* chosen purpose.

So, to summarize what the elements of an optimal purpose statement are:

> " The whole idea behind the 4-Ps Process is to discover what you find energizing and motivating. "

- Choose the one thing that most motivates you and will get you flying out of bed every morning in pursuit of it.
- Select words that are highly specific.
- Choose words that have maximum emotional and visceral meaning to you.
- Keep it short and focused.

As important a step as determining your single purpose is, it is still necessary to take the process of structuring your existence one step further. Therefore, we come to the last of the 4 Ps: selecting appropriate projects to turn your good intentions into *action*.

SELECT AND EXPERIMENT WITH SPECIFIC PROJECTS

If you don't have any shadows, you're not in the light.

—Lady Gaga

Now that you have identified your single, energizing purpose in retirement, it's time to get your butt off the couch and get out there and do something about it! I am mostly kidding; I know you, as a Type A, likely haven't been spending much time lounging about. We Type As are good at getting moving, structuring our days, and accomplishing goals, so this next and final step in the process of selecting specific projects provides a great opportunity to utilize your inherent strengths.

I'm sure most of you already have developed a system over the years for structuring your activities, such as maintaining lists. What self-respecting Type A doesn't have a trusty to-do list handy at all times? Now, you can use your system for keeping organized and on task to implement your purpose and other priorities in retirement.

Making your purpose operational

I had determined that my purpose in life was to be of service, but I still had to make this concept operational. Since family was the highest-priority object of my service, I thought about how I would implement that. The first thing that came to mind was my wife. We love to travel, go to the movies, eat out at nice restaurants, and generally just spend time together. So, now that I'm retired, I am always looking for ways to spend time with her. We aren't "joined at the hip," mind you; we live independent lives most of the time, and we have many interests that do not overlap, which is normal and healthy. Yet, we look for common activities we can share, even simple ones, like agreeing on TV programs we can watch together in the evening. Our many shared interests are a great source of joy. I love her dearly and really enjoy having such a close companion.

To be of service to family and friends, I offer my time and effort whenever they have needs. It might be as simple as helping someone move (although, to protect my back, I let the young people move the really heavy furniture these days!) or as complex as developing a comprehensive retirement plan for one of them. Also, I have organized fun get-togethers that allow us to enjoy each other's company. My wife and I host summer picnics in our backyard, an occasional Christmas cocktail party, a day at the ballpark, and similar family functions. We are lucky to have enough money to help pay for out-of-town vacations that include many of our extended family members and some close friends. This is a great way to spend time together, and everyone seems to appreciate it.

My service to people other than family members and friends has been an interesting road. Trial and error was essential; I tried many different volunteer projects before I found a good fit for me. I had promised myself that I would find a volunteer activity that was not only useful and productive, but also was personally satisfying and fun, which was in keeping with my priority of taking care of and being kind to me. I wasn't going to force myself to do something I didn't like, not in this phase of my life.

> " Trial and error was essential. "

My first attempt was at the local Humane Society. I was excited and hopeful because I love dogs so much. It turned out to be useful and helpful, and I was quite good at it. I was meticulous about taking excellent care of the dogs. I knew that most volunteers on the other shifts didn't walk all of the dogs; there were many dogs, and quite a few were difficult to walk because they were so big and strong. Therefore, I was determined to walk every dog during my shift, and I always did, regardless of the weather. None would get cheated on my watch! I did get some satisfaction from the work, but I also found it a bit isolating, and I had to be honest with myself about that. There were no other humans in the kennel when I helped out, and I discovered that I desired some social interaction as part of my volunteering. So, after nine months or so, I reluctantly moved on to try something else.

Next, I volunteered at a veterans' hospital. I feel strongly about our veterans: they sacrifice so much for all of us and get so little in return. Being somewhat prone to anxiety, I can't even imagine being in a battle or in any sort of life-threatening situation. These men and women have my deepest and utmost respect. With that as motivation, I offered my services to the local veterans' hospital.

Unfortunately, the veterans' hospital had developed very few volunteer positions of any substance; all they could offer me was a job pushing a coffee cart and handing out books. This wasn't a good fit for my high-energy personality. Also, the hospital was very old and poorly maintained, and I found it depressing. Although the veterans were clearly worthy of and deserving of service, the lack of usefulness in my job and the dreary conditions made me unhappy and unlikely to serve well. Again, with much reluctance, I decided to move on.

I had a somewhat poor track record by then. Would I ever find something to keep me busy and productive and happy with my work? Such a volunteer job existed, I was sure; I just needed to persist.

My next attempt was at my local community hospital. People have been volunteering at hospitals for literally centuries, therefore it is a well-developed form of service. I figured that the hospital should have a lot of volunteer positions to choose from, some of which might suit a high-energy, younger person like me. Also, I could socialize with the nurses, doctors, and patients, which would fulfill my need for a social element as part of my work. So, off I went.

Well, as luck would have it, volunteering at my local hospital was a perfect fit. I love it. I found a busy and productive position in the Same Day Surgery Department, where patients come to get minor outpatient surgery. It is a busy area on most days, and, as is the case with most businesses, the employees there (mostly nurses) are overworked. They can use all the help they can get, and I have a lot of energy. I am quite useful, and it is fun to chat with the nurses, anesthetists, doctors, and patients when I have some downtime. Also, I am learning about the health care field, which is new to me, and I find it interesting.

A typical day as a hospital volunteer

You might wonder what I actually *do* all day. That is a good question. The general perception of hospital volunteers is that they are much older workers, candy stripers, if you will, who work in the gift shop. I say this with all due respect to these older volunteers, because I give them a lot of credit for coming to the hospital every day to offer their services in whatever way they can.

Some very busy and physical volunteer work is available if you are so inclined. In Same Day Surgery at my local hospital, along with all of their patient-care responsibilities, the nursing staff is expected to do all of their own stocking of medical supplies, linens, patient snacks and beverages, and the like. They must remove bags of soiled linen and trash to staging areas in the back of the department; strip the linens from, alcohol-wipe, and remake the surgical beds when a patient is finished with it; and discharge patients with a wheelchair to their waiting vehicles in the front of the hospital.

On days when I have enough energy, I perform all of these ancillary duties, greatly lightening the load of the nursing staff. Most important, my work allows the nursing staff to focus all or most of their efforts on patient care. What a huge benefit for them and their patients! And I get to keep my Type A-self busy. It's a win-win.

I get the benefit of some patient contact when I wheel people to their waiting cars and as I bounce around the department carrying out my other duties. I have discovered that I enjoy being around older people, who are the primary patients for outpatient surgery. They have great stories and can be a lot of fun to talk to because of the wisdom of their years.

When I first considered volunteering, I considered it a way to help "others," not family and friends, since I would mostly have contact with strangers. But do you know what I found out? In a short time, the nurses and other employees in my department became some of my best friends. Now I am helping good friends as well as "others" (the patients). It was an unexpected surprise and benefit.

You can benefit even from experiments that don't work

Here is one last example from my experience with selecting projects in retirement. This example demonstrates the value of experimenting and the benefits you can derive even from projects that turn out not to be a good fit.

I love exercise, but especially weightlifting and being in the gym. So, I thought it might be a good idea to become a part-time personal trainer, more for the enjoyment than the pay. I would educate myself more about an area that already interests me and be able to share my passion with others. This idea seemed like it could be a winner.

I studied to become a certified personal trainer, took the certifying exam, and passed it. The study material fascinated me; I learned a lot about weight training and cardiorespiratory conditioning. When I began working in the field, however,

I was disappointed. First, most people want to be trained on weeknights and weekends because they work during the week. This wasn't ideal for me. I already had things I liked to do during these periods, like watch TV and go out socially. I was looking to fill Monday through Thursday from nine a.m. to four p.m. That was my "problem time," not eight o'clock at night when I was winding down to go to bed.

Also, I found the work a bit boring. I enjoyed creating personal workout routines for my clients that took into account any diseases, injuries, or other limitations they had. However, the time I spent in the gym assisting them with their workouts was tedious for me. The work was too slow and plodding for my personality. Besides, to be honest, most of my personal training clients were not very motivated. Many almost expect you to do the work for them or hope you'll perform some magic that will miraculously cause them to shed twenty pounds!

I soon decided that working as a personal trainer didn't suit my high-energy temperament or my desire to do something useful. I enjoyed the learning process, and I did not regret my time spent pursuing this area of interest in any way. In fact, I used my newfound knowledge to significantly change and reenergize my own workout routine, targeting better results. I have been doing this ever since, and it has been fun. I'm in the best shape of my life.

These are a few projects I've worked on since developing a single purpose from my passions and priorities. Some have become part of my daily or weekly routine, which is now quite full. In fact, I have a long list of things that I don't have time to do. If I had more time, I would volunteer more days per week at the hospital. The director of volunteer services is always posting notes in the volunteer office asking for help in other departments if anyone has the time. I also have an interest in volunteering with an organization called SCORE, the Service Corps of Retired Executives, which provides free consulting services to small business that are struggling and can't afford to hire outside help. And I want to get back into playing tennis. I used to play it often when I was younger. It's fun, great exercise, and provides a good social opportunity.

You may have decided on priorities that are relatively unchanging, and hopefully you have been able to identify a primary purpose for your existence in retirement. Still, the ways in which you can implement your priorities and purpose are limitless, constrained only by your imagination. I want to emphasize that the process of identifying potential passions and trying out fun, new projects never needs to stop. Exploring the world for ways to gain experiences and contribute can and should be a lifelong pursuit. It will keep you young, or at the very least, young at heart.

> " The ways in which you can implement your priorities and purpose are limitless, constrained only by your imagination. "

A

EXPAND YOURSELF

 Life moves pretty fast. If you don't stop and look around once in a while, you could miss it.

—Ferris Bueller, *Ferris Bueller's Day Off*

A FUNDAMENTAL SHIFT IN THINKING

Future. That period of time in which our affairs prosper,
our friends are true and our happiness is assured.

—Ambrose Bierce

When I retired I was nervous about what I was going to do for the rest of my life. Understandably so, since I was young to be retired and I'm a high-energy guy. Initially, I responded to my anxiety with a period of non-stop activity in an effort to assuage my fears. For the first two years or so, I allowed my Type A machinery to pretty much run amok.

During this dizzying period, it dawned on me that while the overall approach I had taken toward my life over the previous thirty years had worked well for that phase of my life, at least in terms of attaining wealth and success, it was not a particularly useful approach in retirement. I had grown tired of "the chase." I was frustrated and unhappy. I wanted something different, not just something more. I needed a new paradigm. The attitudes and behaviors that had helped

> " I wanted something different, not just something more. I needed a new paradigm. "

me be so successful in my career were not only mostly useless for what I really desired at this juncture, but they were also possibly counterproductive and harmful. I realized that I needed a significant shift in my thinking if I wanted to fully experience and enjoy this new phase of my life.

I pondered what shifts in thinking would allow me to fully enjoy retirement. What specifically were the ways of thinking that had made me so successful in my career? And now, looking forward, what new and different perspectives would make me happy in retirement? After much thought and analysis, I determined five areas in which I could benefit from a fundamental shift in thinking. The first useful shift was:

Productive, efficient, rushing ▷ Pacing, take your time, rest

When I was busy pursuing my career and parenting, like many Type As, I became a master of time management. If there had been a professional certification available for proficiency in managing my time, I would have earned it with honors! As a workaday Type A in the prime of life, I got more done in a day than anyone would have thought humanly possible. I even surprised myself at times. It was like a game to me, and the prize was based solely on the number of things I could accomplish in a given period.

At work, I was skilled at lasering in on the highest priorities of my job and the most urgent tasks of the day. Then, I would furiously and efficiently multitask until I had completed each of these projects.

Suffice it to say I didn't spend a whole lot of time—or any— standing around the water cooler, shooting the breeze, which was the diversion of choice at that time. Today, it would be texting a buddy about some silly, unimportant detail of my life.

Likewise, when I got home from work, it was a light snack, sweat clothes on, and off to the gym. My usual workout consisted of a one-hour weight-training routine—and surprise, surprise—it was intense. I'd zip back home, have a quick dinner, spend a few minutes with the kids before their bedtime, watch a couple minutes of TV, and fall exhausted into bed.

The next day, rinse and repeat.

The weekends were a bit less hectic, but not by much. On Saturdays, I did another weight-training workout in the morning, errands, and then a social event on Saturday night. Sunday, I read the Bible, worked on home repairs, watched TV at night, and went to bed early for another hard run at the workweek.

In a nutshell, that was my life for about thirty years. I was very focused, productive, and efficient, and as a result, I had accomplished a great deal. Was I enjoying myself? I don't know. I enjoyed the feelings of accomplishment and real or imagined self-worth. Was I happy? I don't think so. I remember often feeling anxious and stressed. But what other choice was there? Slow down and do a mediocre job, which would probably cause me to feel guilty and even more stressed? That didn't seem like a great option.

But at this new point in my life, fully retired from my career and with the kids grown, my only goals would be those I specifically chose for myself. I realized that I could decide to select many challenging goals or fewer, easier ones. What a concept!

Sure, I could decide to do a triathlon and train like a fiend every day in pursuit of it. Or I could start a new business. I could even climb Mt. Everest! Any of these goals would keep me extremely busy and challenged, but what would be the point?

Since there was so little I had to do, why not choose the path of fewer and easier goals? I could take my time with them and actually experience them. What would that hurt? And what if I chose, God forbid, to lay my goals aside for a time and simply rest? All of this might seem obvious to some of you, but when you are used to going a hundred miles per hour with your hair on fire for thirty years, settling down and reflecting on life is not something that first springs to mind!

> " I realized that I could decide to select many challenging goals or fewer, easier ones. What a concept! "

I decided that there was, indeed, not much of a point to maintaining such daunting goals all the time, and eventually I learned how to significantly rest my Type A machinery and get more pleasure out of the activities I chose. I deliberately paced myself, took my time, and rested, and I found much value in it. In later chapters, I will describe specifically how I was able to effect this change in myself.

The second beneficial shift in thinking I discovered was:

Future-oriented, planning ▷ Being present in the moment

The easiest way to bring this concept to life is with a couple of examples.

As you begin your errands, you're standing in line at the grocery store on a Saturday, purchasing a few items. You are thinking about your list for the day, which includes the car wash, dry-cleaner, and hardware store. Like most Type As, you approach this list as if it were a military operation, putting the highest priority on speed and precision. You're going to win this little contest. And then, what does the older fellow in front of you do as he is checking out? He pulls out a fistful of coupons!

He's a "couponer." Oh, no!

This is the worst-case scenario. It will take forever. You'll be way off your timetable by the time he gets it all straightened out, if ever. And, of course, the first coupon is for the forty-eight oz. bottle of laundry detergent, and the gentleman has the twenty-four oz. bottle. How is that going to be reconciled? The store clerk looks dazed and confused about this unexpected turn of events, and now you have gone from being irritated and angry to simply despondent. All is lost!

On Monday, you're at work, and it's the "same old-same old." But you aren't really fully at work because you're thinking about your upcoming Caribbean cruise. Won't that be great! Anything to take your mind off work, right?

Then, ironically, when you actually go on your vacation, you spend much of the time thinking about work. You worry about the projects you must get to, the looming deadlines, etc. To ease your mind, you are wrestling with gaining some measure of control over these thoughts. These are not pleasant, free-floating, vacation-type thoughts! You are denying yourself pleasure on your vacation by uselessly and unnecessarily thinking ahead to being back at work. You are attempting to slay dragons that cannot be slain at that time.

This is an obvious problem and mistake. But did you also consider that you denied yourself any satisfaction that could have been derived from your work while you were focused so longingly on your upcoming vacation? Work can actually have some satisfying elements, but you have to *be there* while they're happening to experience them.

One last example. You're in the middle of your career, raising your kids, doing the whole responsible adult thing, and what do you spend a lot of time thinking about? You're looking ahead to the future when your kids will finally be able to bathe themselves or do their own homework—or better yet, get a damn job and move out! Ah, nirvana!

There is a basic problem with not being mentally where you are physically, as these examples illustrate. We will explore this point in detail later on.

Related to the concept of being in the moment we just discussed is this third idea:

Dissatisfied ▷ Content

Why can't I just enjoy what the heck I'm doing at the time I'm doing it? Why can't I enjoy my current position in life? Why the desire, or need, to be in some future fantasy state or just anywhere else but where I currently am?

This dilemma has at least a little something to do with control. When we're at the grocery store, we're trying to control our whole list of things to do that day, all at once. When we're on vacation, we're trying to control our work, and vice versa.

However, there's even more to it than that. We are continually dissatisfied with where we are rather than focused on whatever good might be available there. We are not very good at experiencing aspects of our present situation that we might enjoy, even relish. It's much easier to trash the present and fantasize about the future, because the future will be great, you just know it! This is a great way to assure that you are never content with where you are or what you have. It's a little sad when you think about it, isn't it?

Let's consider how much more realistic and enjoyable it is to live in the moment. The present is all we have. We will never truly be happy until we reconcile ourselves to the present moment and embrace it. As someone wisely said, "The past is behind us, and the future is forever beyond our grasp." Live here and now. Be grateful. Be grateful for your health, your family, whatever it is you have. And experience the wonderfully satisfying feeling of simply being content.

The fourth shift in thinking I recommend is:

Striving ▷ Existing

While you are in the working phase of your life, your focus tends to be almost exclusively on accomplishing the myriad things that need to be done every day. And rightly so. You have a lot of stuff on your plate. And your goals are important: earning a good living to properly care for your family, raising happy and self-reliant children, taking care of your home, etc. When you retire, however, your schedule will likely be, by design, much less full. At that point, constant striving is no longer a given, a necessity.

Most people are quite familiar with striving. Isn't it what people do all day? It surely is if you are a Type A. But what the heck is this "existing" idea? It might be a bit foreign to you, much as it was to me for most of my life.

I have found a simple way to look at it. Existing is just enjoying who and what you are at any given moment without feeling you have to prove anything, accomplish anything, fill a gap, shore up a weakness, fix something, or become a better or different person. Think of that first moment when you wake up on a weekend morning, before you start to focus on your day. Think of when you first open your eyes and experience the feel of the sheets on your body and the relaxation in your muscles. Maybe you smile a bit, gently stretch, exhale, and decide to fall back to sleep. These moments provide one example of simply existing, of being just for the sake of being.

Your retirement often can be filled with the pleasant experience of simply existing, if you allow it.

The final shift in thinking is:

End result ▷ The "process"

This may be the most important of my five fundamental shifts in thinking to enrich retirement, but it also may be the hardest for Type As to wrap their heads around. Doesn't every activity have a specific purpose, and isn't that the reason you undertake it? Otherwise, why would you be doing it in the first place?

Yes, most goals are based on some purpose, but now that you are retired, why can't that purpose be to enjoy the activity? Why not choose fewer goals and learn how to immerse yourself in them, savor them, and obtain the full experience? Why not relish activities that are part of the simple nature of living: eating breakfast, going for a walk, spending time with family and friends, reading an interesting novel, and so on. You know—just being alive in its simplest form.

> " Maybe, just maybe, life doesn't have to be so damned complicated. "

I am not saying that it is a mistake to have challenging goals in retirement. In fact, as we have found, it can provide its own form of joy. What I am saying is that, in retirement, you have the *option* to do less and experience more. Unlike when you were in the midst of your career, you now have choices.

If there is one thing I've discovered since I've retired, it's that maybe, just maybe, life doesn't have to be so damned complicated. Are we just making it that way?

THE ALL-IMPORTANT ISSUE OF CONTROL

It is better to have self-control than to control an army.

—Proverbs 16:32

Ahhh. Feeling in control. Being in control. Nirvana!

Even a Type A with only a smidgen of self-awareness realizes that control is a central issue: controlling your schedule, trying to control your kids, controlling a project or that difficult subordinate at work, attempting to control your spouse whose needs, wants, and schedule affect your life. It's about controlling anything and everything!

It is also about not being "out of control," the panicky feeling you sometimes get when you're on a plane or an amusement park ride where you're not "in charge." Or maybe your spouse talks you into going to the mall with her and then takes *forever* going into each and every store, which makes you feel oddly anxious, and, of course, irritated.

Why is control so important to us Type As?
How did this come about?

I won't go into great depth here, because I don't think it really matters much how or why we became such control freaks; the methods for counterbalancing it are the same, regardless. Also, I do not profess to expertise in genetics or childhood development. I will say, however, that based on my observations and experience, it certainly seems that the tendency to be controlling can be traced to both inherited traits and learned behavior.

Some young children exhibit unusually high levels of need for orderliness, carefulness, structure, and stability in their environments, while other children of a similar age fling themselves around with abandon because they could not care less about these things. Such variability may indicate that controlling behavior is an inherited trait.

It also appears to be the case that controlling attitudes and behaviors can be learned. Look no further than the example of the child of a severe alcoholic. The chaotic and disordered environment created by an alcoholic can develop a need for a child to seek excessive control in other areas of his or her life, apparently in an effort to compensate.

So, what about the value of being in control? How useful is it?

I view controlling our environment in much the same way as I view achievement and accomplishment. It can be very useful in the right situation and counterproductive in the "wrong" one. At work, maintaining some control over your schedule, duties, and projects is important. You can't just "fly by the seat of your pants" all the time, skipping from task to task with no sense of priorities, and expect to be successful. At play, such as with family or friends, attempting to exert and command too much control can rob you and others of much of the joy of an experience.

Many undesirable consequences can arise from trying too hard to control your environment. Examples are:

- Wasting time and effort and creating unnecessary stress by trying to control trivial things that don't need to be managed so tightly

- Dominating other people, and in the process holding them back from using their full abilities, which marginalizes them and frustrates both of you

- Being unable to fully experience and enjoy an activity

And what about once you are retired? Since, presumably, you will have much less on your schedule, overly controlling behavior can cause you to focus far too much time and effort on minor issues, making mountains out of molehills, so to speak.

What about controlling you instead of your external environment? What about controlling your thoughts, emotions, attitudes, and behaviors?

Controlling your environment versus self-control

This distinction between controlling the environment (including other people) and controlling you is at the heart of the Bible quote at the beginning of this chapter. "Controlling an army" represents controlling all of the people and things around you. Some people do virtually control an army if they hold positions of great power and influence, such as high-level executives and politicians.

"Self-control" means managing and controlling you. This form of control is by far the most important in life. You cannot hope to have any measure of control or positive influence over other people and events until you are stable, steady, manageable, and oriented to the positive. It starts from within. Once you achieve inner control, that's when you can hope to spread its positive effects beyond yourself.

Three levels of control

I have given the issue of how we can achieve effective, realistic, and useful control in our lives a lot of thought, and from this I have developed the concept of three progressive levels of control. By this, I mean three different ways of viewing and attempting to achieve control over yourself and your environment.

Default control

The first level of control is what I've used most of my life. It is the default method of control for Type As who haven't considered the issue. I refer to it as the "illusion of control."

> " Once you achieve inner control, that's when you can hope to spread its positive effects beyond yourself. "

As Type As, we spend most of our waking hours planning, scheduling, and rushing around. When we are in the middle of one activity, we are planning or even mentally "experiencing" the next one. And we are very physically active. Go, go, go all the time. We like the feeling of being in control we get from constant mental and physical activity. It seems reassuring. It gives the mind something to occupy itself at all times. Certainly, we assure ourselves, we must be in control of our fate, because look at how busy and in command of our daily existence we are!

The problem with the illusion of control is that it is just that, an illusion. The lack of control experienced is twofold.

For one, it is not possible to completely control your external environment, no matter how hard you try. Things happen that you do not anticipate or want to happen. On a small scale, I am referring to things like other people being late to a meeting, a store being closed when you arrive, or the common cold descending upon you before a critically important day at work. What you cannot control on a larger scale can be much more devastating, like being injured in a car accident, getting fired, or having a child become terribly ill or a spouse pass away. While you are rushing around under the illusion of complete control, demanding it, any of these events will throw off your gyroscope and be very destabilizing and frustrating.

The second problem with the illusion of control is that we are not really in control of ourselves, our so-called "inner selves," either. When you are constantly busy and occupied, you are avoiding an essential connection to your inner self: your emotions and feelings. For example, a co-worker might say, "You've been working awfully hard lately. You look so tired!" As a Type A, your response likely is, "No, I'm fine. Don't worry." Another example is feeling frustrated with a project and ignoring that feeling because you are so focused on completing the task. For many Type As, getting the job done takes precedence over namby-pamby feelings every day of the week, right? We will explore this concept in more depth in the next chapter, but incessant busyness and lack of connection to your feelings and inner self can cause emotional problems and make it difficult to relax.

If over-planning, over-scheduling, and over-busying yourself is the illusion of control, what is the second, improved level of control for managing your life?

Better and more realistic control

I call this second, improved level "better and more realistic control." It is about being more conscious about the things you do and choosing your actions rather than mindlessly reacting to every situation that presents itself by doing everything that pops into your mind. It also refers to choosing your pace rather than always being frenetic, which is a Type A's somehow comforting default mode. Some days, when you have a lot of responsibilities, you may decide that you feel well and up to them, and you will choose to be very productive. Other days, you may be tired or ill or just feel distracted, frustrated, or sad, and then you may choose to do less. Even on days when you decide to be especially productive, you might skip one or more tasks because they are a lower priority or just because you don't feel like doing them. With this second level of better and more realistic control, you may occasionally take some time out for yourself, just to recoup and relax.

Similar to the idea of making choices based on your feelings, moods, and wants of the moment is being willing and able to adapt to varying circumstances in your external environment. Remember the example of standing in line at the grocery store and watching the person in front of you pull out a grab bag of coupons? At such moments, you can choose to find some joy rather than wallow in frustration and angst. For example, you can people watch. I'm a guy, so if there is even a modestly good-looking woman in line, ogling her discreetly can pleasantly occupy me for a while. Or aren't there always some magazines near the checkout counter? You might flip through the latest copy of *People* magazine, or better yet for us guys, we can troll *Cosmopolitan* or *Shape* for pictures of hot women!

On a larger and more devastating scale, what about the unexpected external circumstance of severe illness of a child, spouse, or other close family member? How do you work that interesting little diversion into your already over-packed schedule? You can simply add it on top of everything else and make a mess of everything, including slighting your sick relative and making yourself miserably frantic. Or, you can choose to do less, which would be more effective and kinder to your unfortunate family member and yourself.

You might be nodding your head right now. "Yes, he has finally discovered what *real and effective* control is." You have discovered the Holy Grail of control!

Well, while the second level of control is "better" than mindlessly reacting and doing whatever presents itself, I have discovered that there actually is a "best" method of control—the third level and final level.

Ironically, it is "relinquishing control."

> " I have discovered that there actually is a 'best' method of control. Ironically, it is 'relinquishing control.' "

Relinquishing control

Yes, giving up the ghost. Not worrying about anything anymore. Just letting it go.

But how can the best form of control be letting go completely? Isn't that the opposite of being in control?

I have found that you can gain access to a tremendous source of comfort, ease, and power by *relinquishing control to God*: surrendering yourself and giving all of your worries to Him. It is, I'll admit, a huge leap of faith, but much faith carries with it many benefits. The Bible says, "Trust the Lord completely. Don't ever trust yourself" (Proverbs 3: 4,5). This is true because, without God's power, we are often weak, misguided, and foolish. With His power, we can do anything.

I'll admit, the first time I tried giving up control, I found it quite unsettling, if not terrifying.

"Let me get this straight," I thought. "I'm going to go to work and let *God* dictate my flow rather than plan out every detail in advance? I'm not going to worry about the presentation I need to do tomorrow?" I wasn't so sure about the wisdom of relinquishing control, to put it mildly.

I want to clarify that giving up control and its close siblings (over-planning, over-scheduling, and over-worry) does not mean giving up being enthusiastic or prepared. It is just a different attitude/mindset that allows for a more positive, relaxed, and productive perspective. You stop running from the devil of fear and potential failure and instead embrace the saint of joy, possibility, and opportunity. *You are no longer afraid*—that is the big difference.

I had to dip my toe in these waters a bit before I gained enough confidence to give up control in my life. Quite honestly, I went through a long period of cycling between giving up control and then nervously taking it back in for a bit! Eventually, however, I learned how to do it consistently and fully, and I was finally at peace with my surroundings, my life, and myself.

> " You are no longer afraid— that is the big difference. "

Some people refer to this idea as "Let go, let God." You might think of it as being like a child: vulnerable, flexible, spontaneous, and trusting. That is the mindset. I have found that it is easier to achieve this state if you lower your expectations for yourself and your life (go easy on yourself and give yourself a break), don't care what other people think of you (put down your guard), and love and accept yourself "as is," with no conditions or qualifications.

The joy of living your life with no worries and God at the helm is tremendous. It's like being set free, fully able to enjoy and experience life. Since you will no longer be so worried about the future, you can live in the present moment, savoring every detail of every experience. That's living!

Think of this analogy. I happen to take very, very good care of my dog because I love the little fella so much and he relies on me. I attend to his every need, whether it's for food, water, shelter, recreation, doing his business outside, or whatever. And when I think of God, I imagine and truly believe that He takes care of me one hundred times (a million times?) better than I take care of my little dog. He loves me that much! When you really believe like this, it is comforting, *completely* comforting.

Some people have argued that the benefit you derive from giving up control is only the result of being able to free up your creative machinery and not worry, and that it has nothing to do with God. Yes, it's true, if you are, say, about to give a presentation to a roomful of people and you decide you don't really care about the outcome, you generally will do a much better job because your natural abilities will flow out of you, unrestrained by worry, concern, self-consciousness, and the like. But there is more to it than that. There is more power available; much more if you are willing to tap into it. It is not just a matter of eliminating a "negative." It is a matter of accessing a huge and unfathomably positive force and source of energy.

I will offer one last analogy to illustrate my concepts about control.

Let's say you were asked to hold a small stone in your hand for as long as possible. Picture it. At first, you grasp the stone with your palm face down, squeezing with all your might. Soon, you realize that you won't be able to sustain a firm hold for long, so you loosen your grip a bit. Yet, it still takes a lot of energy to hold the stone in that position. And then you realize, "Aha! If I place the stone in my hand with my palm facing up, not gripping but simply cradling it, it is much easier and more comfortable, and I might even be able to hold it this way forever!"

You might think of this example as you address the issue of control in your life.

THE SIMPLE KEY TO BEING ABLE TO RELAX

Patience is the ability to idle your motor when you feel like
stripping your gears.

—Barbara Johnson

I wondered about relaxation for most of my adult life. I read many
books. I brought up the subject with family members and friends.
God knows, I analyzed and turned it over in my mind an infinite
number of times. I never found a good explanation, one that
answered the question at its deepest and most fundamental level.

Why can't I relax?

It seems so simple, so basic. You just sit down and relax,
right? Some people are able to do it with such ease. They do it
throughout the day and every day. It is a routine part of their
existence and comes naturally to them.

I couldn't seem to do it at all, at least not fully and consistently.
Why was that?

I had always been good at everything I put my mind to. I'd
been able to conquer almost everything else in life that I'd set my
sights on. I had achieved a fine education, excelled at my career,
raised a family, kept myself in outstanding physical condition—

you name it. If I could achieve all this, why couldn't I conquer an apparently simple activity? It was a mystery, wrapped in an enigma, shrouded in secrecy.

A couple of years into retirement, while attending a self-help seminar led by a couple of therapists, I figured what the heck, I'm going to ask my same tired, old question one more time. I did not have high hopes that I would learn anything new.

"I am a Type A person who is constantly busy," I said, "and I just can't seem to relax. Why is that?"

One of the therapists casually responded, "Oh, that's easy. I've worked with many people like you, and I can tell you exactly why."

To say that she had my attention is an understatement! "Please do tell me why."

After hearing her explanation, I knew I had finally found the answer I was seeking.

Here is what she told me.

Ignore them and they'll go away doesn't apply to feelings

Type As busy themselves and rush around all the time. Through their constant physical and mental activity, they ignore or avoid their feelings and emotions. Their busyness distracts them from whatever they are feeling in the moment, and these are often negative and uncomfortable feelings that inevitably arise in everyone from time to time: frustration, disappointment, anger, jealousy, insecurity, tiredness, boredom, and so on. When such feelings are not addressed, they remain unresolved.

Over time, unaddressed feelings and emotions get pent-up, sometimes for days or weeks or more, depending on how long they are ignored. They won't just go away; they will need to be addressed at some point. Like floodwaters accumulating against a dam, the water builds up more and more pressure until it overwhelms the dam or the pressure is released.

When you eventually stop busying yourself and sit still, which must happen at some point, the unexpressed feelings and emotions come to the fore. Because you are not distracted but rather focused on and aware of yourself, your mind begins processing the pent-up feelings. Especially if you have allowed yourself to de distracted for a long time, the resulting flood of emotions is likely to produce a strong sense of anxiety. You may feel quite uncomfortable, mentally and emotionally.

> " Over time, unaddressed feelings and emotions get pent-up. Like floodwaters accumulating against a dam, the water doesn't go away. "

Predictably, people often react to the intense and uncomfortable feelings by busying themselves again. While getting busy is a relief in the short run, it simply postpones the inevitable issue of having to deal with and process these feelings.

I listened intently and thought, "Wow! I think she's right. In fact, I know she's right. This is what has been happening to me for years."

This was why, when I sat down at the end of the day to relax, often I scanned the environment for something that needed to be cleaned, fixed, or straightened and immediately jumped up and did it.

I asked the critical and obvious next question: "What is the solution? What can I do differently so that I can overcome the problem and be able to truly relax?"

Why sitting with feelings is crucial for Type As

She said the solution was quite simple—simple, but not necessarily easy, especially at first when you are not accustomed to doing it.

When you slow down or stop and the inevitable flood of feelings and emotions washes over you, *just sit there. Sit with your emotions.* You may experience an even fuller rush of feelings, depending on how long you have been ignoring them, but just let it happen. *Feel it. Experience it.* It's okay! These feelings are normal; they are not dangerous. You'll live. And, eventually, you will come to grips with them and become more comfortable, peaceful, and relaxed.

If it helps, you can focus for a while on your breathing. Take deep breaths, in and out. Wait patiently, and you will find your core of calm.

The therapist told me that Type As need to learn how to get their emotions under control in order to learn how to relax and be comfortable during times when nothing is planned. They have to believe that they can handle and rein in their emotions.

She said that if we can be aware of and process our feelings throughout the day, even as we are busy with our various tasks, all the better. Then we will have fewer pent-up feelings to address when we eventually slow down or stop.

Finally, the answers I had been seeking!

Oh, and that "idiot" psychiatrist who several years earlier had kept asking me, "And how does that make you feel?" Well, maybe I should have listened to him!

You might ask whether most of us Type As are simply *ignoring* our feelings, or are we consciously *avoiding* our feelings? Which is it? There is a difference, right?

I don't think this distinction is very important in the long run, because the result is the same; for pent-up and unresolved feelings, the solution is the same. It may be that some Type As are anxiety-prone, which might lead them to avoid their feelings since any negative feelings make them anxious and uncomfortable. On the other hand, many Type As are just high-energy people who don't spend much time processing their feelings simply because they have chosen goals and tasks that they consider more important. As a result, they ignore their feelings.

> " Feel it.
> Experience it.
> It's okay! These feelings are normal; they are not dangerous. You'll live. And, eventually, you will come to grips with them and become more comfortable, peaceful, and relaxed. "

A final note about relaxing and staying in touch with your feelings: you can practice and learn!

In pursuit of this highly worthwhile goal, we will next explore how to quiet your mind.

QUIETING YOUR MIND

All men's miseries derive from not being able to sit in a quiet room alone.

—Blaise Pascal

What does it mean to "quiet your mind," and why is it so helpful?

Unbeknownst to most of us, our minds are constantly involved in an internal dialogue. For Type As, with our limitless energy, this is especially true. Have you ever taken the time to monitor your inner dialogue? The thoughts that flash through our minds throughout the day are both revealing and fascinating.

When people talk about retirement, they often say they want to travel and explore the world. Some people make exploring the depths of the ocean or outer space their life's work. Exploring your mind can be just as interesting. There's much to be discovered about your inner self.

How your thoughts dictate your life

For some reason, much of what we occupy our minds with, unconsciously or semi-consciously, is negative. As it says in the Bible, "It is the thoughtlife that pollutes" (Mark 7:20). I'm not sure why this is so, except that our insecurities must trump any optimism we have. Maybe it's because, "The bad stuff is easier to believe," as Julia Roberts' character states in the movie *Pretty Woman*. This is unfortunate, because thoughts, conscious or not, dictate attitude, mood, and behavior.

> " Along with the negative thoughts and insecurities that plague both Type As and Type Bs, Type As also occupy their minds with things like over-planning, over-analyzing, and judging. "

Along with the negative thoughts and insecurities that plague both Type As and Type Bs, Type As also occupy their minds with things like over-planning, over-analyzing, and judging.

"When I get started on that new project next week, I'll need to get sales and the plant people involved. I'd better call them first thing Monday morning."

"That party tonight was a disaster, wasn't it? There were only ten people there, nothing good to drink, and the food was cold. What were they thinking?"

"That guy in front of me is a terrible driver. He's all over his lane and mine. Who's driving that car, Stevie Wonder?"

The Type A mind is filled with this chatter.

Programming based on past experiences

Most internal dialogue consists of "programming" we've developed over the years based on past experiences, particularly our reactions to those experiences. We react to events and people in a habitual way. For example, let's say that you and your spouse are planning a visit with your sister and brother-in-law. You're dreading it. Your unconscious mind replays your past reactions:

"Tom is always so negative and pessimistic. This is going to be really painful."

Multiple problems arise when you bring your past reactions into your present experience. First, predetermining the outcome of an event puts you into a sour mood well before the event has even happened. You don't need to do this. It just frustrates and irritates you when you are engaged in other activities, say, walking the dog, which otherwise could have been pleasant. And then, when you actually do visit your relatives, your pessimistic attitude makes it more likely that you will, in fact, create the condition you are dreading. Why?

Think about it. Your negativity is bound to be reflected in your posture, in the amount of eye contact you make, in your tone of voice, and in your choice of words. From the very outset of the experience, your non-verbal and verbal cues will be flashing to your brother-in-law: "I'm uncomfortable. I don't like you. I want to get out of here." Well, don't you think the response you get from him will be similarly negative and unfriendly? Even if he doesn't pick up on your negative cues and reciprocate, you will be so focused on what you expect to see that any little thing he does will justify your expectations and confirm for you that he is, indeed, insufferable. In other words, you will "see" what you expect to see. "Look at how Tom gave me that smirk. I knew he was an ass!" This reinforces your judgment, stokes your anger, and encourages you to continue demonstrating your hostility toward him, which only sets you up for another negative attitude and experience the next time you see him.

You can see how the cycle perpetuates itself.

However, what if you approached the visit differently? I'm not necessarily talking about an unrealistically positive attitude, just a somewhat neutral approach, a "let's see what happens" attitude. Well, making this small shift could change everything. You won't be ruining the walk with your dog beforehand by dwelling on all those expected negative outcomes. When you arrive at the event, you will not be flashing all those negative signals. And lo and behold, you may discover that Tom is actually being a pretty good guy that day. Will wonders never cease! You may actually have a pleasant visit.

Let's say that the next time you plan to see Tom, you again approach the visit with a neutral attitude. However, this time, Tom is being somewhat irritating. Well, that can happen. But you have still saved yourself a lot of grief and suffering by not anticipating this outcome and reinforcing it.

Programming is a problem because it tends to be negative, and it chains us to the past. It keeps us from experiencing situations in a pure and free manner. Our negative inner dialogue about past experiences sets up a din in our heads that makes it difficult to live in and enjoy the present. And I mean the "real" present, not our preconceived and often somewhat distorted notion of the present. How likely is it that we can relax and be at peace when we pre-program? Not very.

How to stop habitual negative thinking

So what to do? How do we stop the continuous noise and habitual negative thinking that go on in our minds?

The simplest method is to take time out of each day for "quiet time." This involves finding a quiet spot somewhere in your house and taking a breather from your busy day. No TV, no reading material, nothing. Just sitting alone, quietly, with your thoughts. This is a not a common practice for most Type As.

To help you relax as you sit there quietly, you might focus for a while on your breathing. Take nice, even, slow breaths, in and out. As you exhale, imagine your mind and body relaxing further and more deeply. This is also a good opportunity to relax the muscles in your neck, which tighten up during the course of a busy day. Slowly roll your head around and around, stretching your neck muscles more fully with each rotation. This can be especially relaxing because it focuses your mind on your body and its sensations, diverting you from your mental chatter and thereby helping to quiet your mind.

What's the usefulness here? For many Type As, the initial experience will be frustrating and seem pointless. However, if you give it enough time and open yourself up to the experience, it will gradually become quite the opposite. Eventually, it will feel pleasurable, reassuring, and stabilizing. Instead of that initial feeling of being "out of control" as you ignore your schedule for a while, soon the opposite feeling of empowerment will begin to well up inside. You might begin to realize that you don't need to be running around all the time. Actually, being able to sit there quietly for a few minutes proves to you that your tasks are not so important that the world will crumble if you divert your attention for a moment. You don't need to be a slave to your schedule. You actually feel more in control of yourself while sitting there quietly than when you were so busy reacting to all of the demands your mind makes on you. Why? Because you have made a *conscious choice* to sit there quietly, proving to yourself that you can, in fact, stop for a while and all will still be well.

I must admit, even with the pleasurable sensation that comes from sitting quietly, *every single time* I think about taking time out to do it, my initial reaction is reluctance. That is probably because I have been such a long-time, habitual Type A, and I have an entrenched idea that I can easily go on without taking any time out for myself. Yet, it is also true that *every single time* I do take some quiet time, I enjoy it immensely and find it rewarding. It might seem paradoxical, but I think it is simply because long-term Type A attitudes and behaviors are difficult to change.

Balancing an overactive body and mind

Hopefully, as you continue to spend time alone with your thoughts, eventually you will discover the sensation of true relaxation. Sitting quietly is an important balancing mechanism for our overactive bodies, which are constantly working, cleaning, fixing, and rushing. It also brings balance to our overactive Type A minds, which are always analyzing, judging, worrying, and planning.

> " Quiet time is also an opportunity to let your feelings and emotions catch up with your body. "

Quiet time is also an opportunity to let your feelings and emotions catch up with your body. As discussed in the last chapter, the key to being able to really relax is to occasionally "interrupt" your busy existence so you can reconnect to whatever feelings and emotions you have been setting aside during your busy day.

What is this *feeling* thing?

There is another issue, though. As Type As, we may be so unaccustomed to examining our feelings that they seem unfamiliar and hard to discern. "What is this whole *feeling* thing? What types of feelings might I experience, and what sensations accompany them? I just feel vaguely anxious and uncomfortable, and I don't particularly like it."

Well, it turns out that someone out there is quite perceptive about this whole issue of feelings, and she has developed a tool to help us identify and differentiate our feelings. Dr. Gloria Willcox of St. Petersburg, Florida, created something called the "Feeling Wheel." You can view it on my website at *Type-A-Lifestyle. com/the-feeling-wheel*. The wheel shows a broad spectrum of possible human feelings and emotions. The top half of the wheel identifies negative emotions, such as mad, angry, and irritated, while the bottom half details positive emotions, like peaceful, trusting, and relaxed. As you progress from the innermost circle of the wheel to the outer bands, the feelings described are more nuanced. It can be interesting and illuminating to spend some quiet time looking over this diagram. Reconciling yourself to experiencing natural human feelings and emotions is a critical step toward finding peace with yourself and feeling comfortable in your own skin.

Eventually, you should be able to carry the sense of stillness and peacefulness you find during quiet times over into some of your daily activities, allowing you to fully experience each thing you do with a peaceful and relaxed mind.

For those of you who are intrigued by the concept of quieting your mind and exploring your inner self and who are willing to invest even more time and effort into achieving its benefits, I offer you what I believe to be the best and most beneficial form of meditation I have ever encountered. It is called Vipassana meditation.

VIPASSANA MEDITATION

To enjoy good health, to bring true happiness to one's family, to bring peace to all, one must first discipline and control one's own mind.

— Buddha

Vipassana meditation is a brilliant method for calming the mind. I have practiced it for years and found it hugely beneficial. Since it requires a fair amount of time and effort, retirement is a great time to learn it. It's both interesting and kind of fun.

An outstanding treatment of the subject is *Vipassana Meditation as Taught by S. N. Goenka,* written by William Hart. It provides very clear explanations and interesting and thought-provoking examples. What follows in this chapter is based on the principles outlined in Hart's book.

A basic principle of Vipassana meditation is that the mind tends to react to experiences and events with either liking or disliking. As an example, when you eat ice cream, since the sensation of eating it is pleasurable, your mind reacts with "liking." Conversely, if you attend a social event and it bores you, which is not a pleasurable sensation, you react by "disliking" it. All your reactions of liking and disliking are stored in your subconscious memory for future reference.

All of us are continually experiencing events and reacting to the sensations they evoke with liking or disliking. The result is that we form ingrained, automatic reactions in our minds that we recall unconsciously whenever we encounter the same or similar experiences in the future.

Vipassana meditation teaches that these ingrained reactions are harmful to us. All of this conditioning creates craving for things we like and aversion to those we dislike. We then spend most of the day in the mental states of craving and aversion. While we are eating dinner, we crave our favorite dessert. When we are finally eating the dessert, we are averse to the idea that the pleasure will end and try to hold onto it too tightly. When we are watching TV during the week, we have aversion to it if, instead, we crave having our usual Saturday night drinks at a bar. When we are at work, we crave a vacation.

So, we spend most of our time not experiencing the present, but rather being averse to it while craving other, more pleasurable experiences that aren't available in the present moment. And we cannot fully enjoy pleasurable experiences because we are frustrated by their temporary nature.

Experiences you like actually can be harmful if you view or interpret them with a lot of emotion. Certainly, developing much liking for something that is dangerous to you, like using drugs, is obviously bad. But even liking something good for you, such as certain people, events, or material things, is still harmful because, if you become too attached to them, you will spend much time craving them when they are not available. This naturally produces aversion for your current state, which robs you of enjoying the present.

Vipassana meditation teaches that the problem with being attached to things we like and feeling aversion for things we dislike is twofold: not only does it lead to constant craving and aversion, but since everything in our world is constantly changing and impermanent, becoming attached to anything is folly. I love my spouse dearly, but she can be taken away in an instant due to an accident or some medical calamity, like an aneurysm or heart attack. I really like my house, but it can be quickly destroyed by fire; and if you take the long view, at some future date it will be torn down and no longer exist. Being overly attached to people or things is based on the unrealistic assumption that they will always be there for you.

> " A classic idea associated with Vipassana meditation is that it is better to treat all things as impermanent, which is reality and which allows you to fully enjoy them in the moment. "

A classic idea associated with Vipassana meditation is that it is better to treat all things as impermanent, which is reality and which allows you to fully enjoy them in the moment. This is referred to as "viewing the glass as broken." It means that the best way to fully and joyfully experience a favored thing is to cultivate the viewpoint that, eventually, it will no longer exist. We should enjoy it for what it is now and not be too attached to it, with the realistic understanding that eventually it will be gone. For example, I can and should fully enjoy my spouse right now, without expecting a future that is not assured.

Vipassana meditation also teaches that some mental conditioning is so deep and permanent that it can be especially harmful. When you experience things with little or no associated emotion, they do not create very strong conditioning and therefore they are not as harmful. For instance, when you go to a movie and dislike it, you may become mildly conditioned to view certain types of movies or particular actors in a negative way. This kind of negative conditioning is innocuous and will likely disappear from the subconscious quickly because it was not very deeply felt.

But what about a child who is required to make a presentation in front of the class when the child is too young and/or does not possess the necessary capabilities to handle something so difficult. Let's say the child does not feel well that day, which makes the request even more daunting. During the presentation, the child becomes extremely nervous, stammers, is terribly embarrassed, and runs back to his seat in tears. This is a severely traumatizing situation. The child may be paralyzed by the prospect of speaking in front of others for the rest of his life. This one very difficult experience may even lead to stunted social skills.

Mild conditioning is like a ripple in a pond that quickly dissipates or a line drawn in the sand that is soon erased by the wind. But a traumatic experience cuts deeply into the psyche, as though etched in stone.

Since everything in our world is constantly changing both around and within us, and since one event does not necessarily predict the future, why should anyone be "sentenced" like this? Is it necessary? No, in fact, it is not. When this child becomes an adult and develops an open and unconditioned mind, which can be achieved with Vipassana meditation, he may very well turn out to be an accomplished and comfortable public speaker. Vipassana meditation teaches you how to unchain yourself from the past and use your full talents and abilities to take advantage of the present. Once you begin to explore this idea fully, it can be life-changing.

The process and practice of Vipassana meditation

How do we achieve these beneficial results? What is the actual process and practice of Vipassana meditation?

There are two phases to Vipassana meditation. The first is the attainment of *concentration*, and the second is immodestly but rightfully called the attainment of *wisdom*.

The attainment of concentration

To develop improved concentration, sit in a relaxed way, in a quiet place, and simply focus your entire attention on your breathing. Direct all of your attention toward the simple process of breathing in and breathing out. You are not to think about how long you might sit there, your next task for the day, or anything else.

You might think it sounds ridiculously simple. Why even bother? "I can master that easily."

Well, in fact, it turns out to be extremely difficult. As you sit there, your mind runs off in all sorts of directions, much like a spoiled child.

> " As you sit there, your mind runs off in all sorts of directions, much like a spoiled child. "

"Oh, I forgot about that dry-cleaning I need to pick up!"

"I wonder what's on TV tonight."

"This posture I'm in is a little uncomfortable."

"I wonder why that clerk was so short with me. Did I say something to upset her?"

Vipassana teaches that this continual internal dialogue is quite common. A constant stream of thoughts runs through our minds, preventing us from experiencing any peace. In meditation, every time your mind wanders from your breath to some other worry or concern, Vipassana teaches you to gently return your concentration to your breathing.

At first, you might be able to hold your concentration on your breathing for a few seconds, only to be whisked away by your mind to somewhere else. After several sessions of practice, you develop the ability to concentrate for longer intervals, having learned to concentrate on the present moment without all of the usual mental clutter and distraction.

Why is concentration so important, especially to Type As? Because our minds are constantly churning and racing; specifically, Type As worry needlessly and helplessly about matters that cannot be addressed in the moment. This is unnecessary suffering.

Also, "As goes the mind, so goes the body." If your mind is running off in all directions, what are you probably doing physically? Rushing around, right?

The attainment of concentration is essential to any sort of peace for a Type A in retirement. You will not be able to fully relax and gain the benefit of your experiences without it.

The attainment of wisdom

The second, and ultimate, goal of Vipassana meditation is the attainment of wisdom. Since a full discussion of this topic is too complicated to entertain here, I will briefly summarize it for you. The attainment of wisdom involves eradicating your mind of all past conditioning. Being free of past conditioning allows you to experience events as they actually are and the world as it truly is. Realizing that the world is constantly changing and impermanent enables you to value that which *is*—reality, and the present moment—fully and completely.

If you are intrigued by Vipassana meditation, which I hope you are, I encourage you to read Hart's book on the subject. It is a quick read, and I think that, as a Type A, you'll find the principles and stories fascinating.

In the spirit of full disclosure, if you haven't figured this out already, Vipassana meditation is based on Buddhist principles. You might say, "I'm not becoming a Buddhist, I can tell you that right now!"

Yes, the origins of Vipassana are Buddhist, however William Hart's treatment of it actually contains very little of a sectarian nature. I have found this form of meditation to be quite consistent with and supportive of my Christian beliefs. People of any religious faith can do it without compromise. In fact, it should only enhance your spirituality.

In closing, and with all due respect to other religions, I must say that the Buddhists know an awful lot about meditation. They have probably forgotten more about meditation than many of us will ever know!

LET GO OF INTELLECTUAL VANITY

Cruelty is, perhaps, the worst kind of sin.
Intellectual cruelty is certainly the worst kind of cruelty.

—Gilbert K. Chesterton

Based on my own behavior and that of the many Type As I have contact with daily, I have observed one thing that we Type As prize above all else: being right. In almost any discussion, it is extremely important to us that others validate our intellectual position.

It goes something like this: The Type A interjects into a discussion: "Sorry (spouse/friend/co-worker/neighbor), but I'm *certain* about this, and I'll tell you why." Or, "No, no, no! Now, listen to me, and I'll explain why you're wrong. Blah, blah, blah."

> " I have observed one thing that we Type As prize above all else: being right. "

This scenario plays out all day, every day, across our great land.

When we are working, it is somewhat useful to hold strong positions on important, work-related issues. Type As, especially, want to be considered knowledgeable. This is true for Type As in supervisory or leadership positions, which many are because they are aggressive and ambitious. However, it is also true even when Type As are in roles that emphasize technical knowledge and expertise. This desire to be seen as smart is only natural, and it can be a positive thing—up to a point. By this, I mean that it is useful short of your being an insufferable "know it all," in which case your fellow workers will likely avoid you at all costs.

But let's say you have retired. What will be your demeanor in this new phase of life? In retirement, the vain need to be right all the time can be particularly unhelpful, and even damaging. Instructing others because of your need for intellectual validation can be harmful to the person you are instructing, who may often feel belittled, marginalized, and agitated. It can also be detrimental be to you, the person doing the instructing or criticizing, because it causes unnecessary mental agitation.

Here is an example. I have a friend whose husband is an extremely strong-willed Type A, whereas she is more of a Type B. Below is a recent discussion that occurred between them.

It was wintertime, and when they arrived back home after being away on vacation, they discovered it was colder in their house than it should have been. The husband immediately went and checked the thermostat, which happened to be the newer digital type, and saw that the screen was blank. Upon seeing this, he told his wife, "Something's wrong with the thermostat. I need to call the heating and air people to come and fix it."

His wife responded, "Oh, are you sure, honey? I think it might just need a new battery."

Her comment implied that she was questioning her husband's judgment that they required the expertise of professionals.

For a Type A like him, this was an unacceptable affront to his intellectual prowess. Gird for war!

In a very firm and condescending tone, he replied, "There's no battery in this thing. These thermostats are wired into the electricity!"

"Whatever you say, dear."

The husband called the local heating and air company. His wife was able to hear her husband's part of the conversation. He explained the problem to the technician, and upon hearing their response, he muttered something to the effect of, "Oh, really? Is that right? Okay. Thanks for your help," and hung up the phone.

I don't need to tell you what the problem with the thermostat was.

Ooops!

This is an example of an aggressive Type A taking a firm stance on an issue and being proved wrong. You might say, "Yes, I can be pretty adamant about certain issues, but only when I'm right, so that makes it acceptable."

Hmm. Well, let's explore a scenario in which the intellectual aggressor is, in fact, correct, or at the very least has an arguably useful point to make. Might being so aggressively instructive still do damage?

In this case, it happened to be me. Initially, I intended to instruct someone, but I held back at the last second. Since this was such a rare situation in which I was both "right" in some fashion *and* didn't choose to immediately correct the other person, I knew I needed to include the example in my book!

The front door of our home had developed a slight problem. It no longer closed tightly, which allowed unwanted cold or hot air to enter our house. To fix it, I added a piece of weather stripping along the doorjamb. Both my wife and I agreed it was an improvement. The only small problem now was that the door closed a bit too tightly, which made it difficult to operate the lock.

After the repair, my wife struggled a great deal while trying to open the lock, violently turning the key back and forth. This is probably an exaggeration (of the Type A variety), but it seemed to me that she would endlessly work the key back and forth.

I found having to regularly observe her process frustrating, to put it mildly.

For whatever reason, my wife had found little need to give the matter much thought. You can hardly blame her, since it was not exactly a problem of epic proportions. But I, a diligent Type A, felt it was a situation that had to be addressed, partly because it bothered me so much, and also because Type As like me love to solve problems, especially if that creates "order" in our lives.

I spent some "quality time" with the door and lock and determined that it unlocked quite easily from the outside if you pulled the door toward you as you turned the key, because this would relieve the pressure on the lock where it inserts into the doorjamb. Likewise, if you were locking the door from the inside, pushing forward on the door would allow the lock to operate easily.

So what to do with this information? What I had discovered would have been a somewhat useful tip, but let's face it, my wife could take it as criticism, especially if I delivered it in the wrong fashion. In the old days, had I observed her again struggling with the lock, I immediately would have barked out something on the order of "For #$&* sake! What the hell are you doing over there? You're going to damage the lock!" (For the uninitiated, this is a bad thing for your relationship.) And then I would have instructed her, in the most demeaning voice I could muster, how simple it was to unlock the door if she had just given it at least a moment's thought, and upon which I would show her the masterful way in which *I* opened the door!

Luckily, being a moderately reformed Type A, I resisted saying any of this. Whew, that was a close call!

Have you noticed what these two examples have in common? Both involve issues that are quite trivial, as most arguments between spouses and friends do.

Does it matter very much whether the thermostat is directly wired into the electrical system or powered by a battery? And how about the most efficient way to lock and unlock a door that fits a bit too snugly? Are these issues worthy of strong emotion or a confrontation? Are they worth risking someone's self-esteem or peaceful mood?

While disagreements over trivial issues often have a clear winner and loser (but then who cares?), for issues that are really important, usually it is instead the case that neither position can be judged as entirely right or wrong. These tend to be matters of opinion or personal preference. Therefore, neither trivial issues nor more serious matters are really worth being overly adamant or conceited about.

For example, important issues that might arise between spouses are things like childrearing, money, sex, and family relationships. I'm sure you can see that these are more about opinions and preferences than they are about facts. So, while it is critical to thoroughly discuss them and reach some consensus or agreement, it is not helpful to enter into such a discussion with the goal of dominating your spouse and "winning" the argument.

> " Intellectual vanity is not helpful for either small, trivial issues or for more serious and consequential ones. "

No matter how vehemently you argue your position, you are not likely to ever prove your spouse wrong because of the subjective nature of the issue. It is more likely that you will only antagonize and marginalize him or her and cut off any future discussion. This is not much of a "win."

Two other examples of serious and weighty issues that have no winner or loser are the universally taboo social topics of religion and politics. Both are quite important, but it should be understood that it is useless to pursue the goal of arriving at a "correct" answer or any sort of agreement in matters such as these.

I think we can conclude, then, that intellectual vanity is not helpful for either small, trivial issues or for more serious and consequential ones.

The desire or need to always be right was labeled "intellectual validity" many decades ago by a perceptive medical doctor. In 1950, Dr. Abraham Low published a seminal book entitled, *Mental Health through Will-Training*; unfortunately, he passed away shortly thereafter. The book described his concept of intellectual validity in detail, along with a number of other interesting concepts. I became aware of Dr. Low's book and its use as an aid to help people who suffer from anxiety, as I did at the time.

Here is an excerpt from Dr. Low's book:

> I shall now give you a brief account of the intellectual mentality…. His stock is the insistence, repeated tirelessly and ruthlessly, that he is right, that you better take his advice, that he could have told you how to avoid trouble if you had only cared to listen to him. Thinking that he is right, he promptly assumes that the others are wrong. Hence, he delights in correcting the statements and opinions of those about him. He is critical, aggressive, meddlesome…. Enjoying a self-appointed monopoly in correct thinking, he is eager to mend and 'reform' the defective thought processes of others…. The essence of his attitude is that he knows and is right and that the others are ignorant and wrong. And if they are wrong, it is his duty to tell them (p. 78).

Dr. Low uses the term *intellectual validity* to describe pride in one's views, opinions, plans, and decisions. I prefer to refer to it as *intellectual vanity*, which I believe is more descriptive. Dr. Low even refers to this behavior as a form of vanity.

What is so unnecessary or harmful about intellectual vanity? Dr. Low states that the exchange of claims and counterclaims is but a pretense that only creates tension and ill will to no benefit. He describes it as "…a matching of wits in which the question at issue [is]: Who knows better? Whose is the superior intelligence?…To admit one's limitations is humility, to insist on one's superior knowledge is vanity. With a humble awareness of [one's] average limitations, [your] body is in repose and [your] mind at peace" (p. 163).

How does a Type A person who is prone to intellectual vanity limit or stop this behavior? I can tell you it is not easy, because I have been a serial offender and struggled mightily with this behavior throughout my life. I developed an effective tool to "catch myself" before I launch into some tirade of correcting someone or engaging in a battle of wits, whether it is over something trivial or important, and I'll share it with you.

One day, I wrote down all the areas of knowledge I am weak in; these included not only technical areas, but also emotional ones. At the outset, I knew I needed to be very honest with myself if I wanted the exercise to have any usefulness. It was an embarrassingly long list that included: mechanical equipment of any kind (car, boat, furnace, garage door opener—anything with a motor); foreign affairs; geography; child-rearing; computer hardware; fishing and hunting; world religions; women; local government; cooking and housecleaning; medicine; teaching; basic social graces; and so on. And I was just getting started. Ouch!

So, the moment I get the urge to correct, criticize, or display my superior knowledge in an area, I think, "Okay, I may or may not be an expert or more knowledgeable about this than the person I'm speaking to, but even if I am, there are a zillion other things I am not good at, things this person probably knows more about than I do. So, be kind. Maybe I know a lot about this, but there is plenty I don't know, so be humble."

This seems to help me, especially when coupled with the observation that, from an emotional standpoint, correcting someone harshly does much more harm than good.

Perhaps you will benefit from performing this simple exercise. I can say with much certainty that your spouse, relatives, and friends will really appreciate it.

PEACE VERSUS EXCITEMENT

Imagine that the universe is a great spinning engine. You want to stay...
right in the hub...not out at the edges where all the wild whirling takes
place, where you can get frayed and crazy.

—Elizabeth Gilbert

From a broad perspective, intellectual vanity can be considered a form of mental excitement. It is energizing to display our superior intellect and vast storehouse of knowledge to all who will listen, isn't it?

From what I have observed, not only are we Type As prone to intellectual vanity, but also, in general, we like excitement. We crave the feeling of it—it makes us feel alive. Excitement also gives us an outlet for releasing our seemingly limitless energy.

What types of excitement do Type As favor?

I have touched on some of them before. Seeking intellectual validation and rushing around are forms of excitement. In addition to indulging in intellectual vanity, we Type As love our to-do lists, and nothing gives us more satisfaction than to get a list accomplished in record time, even while tossing in a few extra tasks along the way.

We also seem to enjoy being exceptional, which is related to intellectual vanity and rushing around. At work or school, pursuing and attaining exceptional performance can be worthwhile. However, its value is more questionable when we are doing our weekend errands, attending a social event, or playing a game, for example.

In social settings, Type As usually try too hard to be perceived as exceptional and "perfect," which we find exciting. Some of us can be a bit insecure at times, so at parties we might be found boasting unnecessarily of our accomplishments and successes. This attitude of exceptionality and being better than others is not impressive, as we hope it will be; it is off-putting and not at all attractive. People prefer to socialize and spend time with people who are open, vulnerable, and human. It makes them feel more comfortable and at ease.

Activities like alcohol and drug abuse, excessive gambling, and preoccupation with pornography attract people who are excitement-prone, and they can be very harmful.

What is wrong with pursuing excitement?

For one, the exciting activity will naturally run its course and come to an end, as must all things, and once again we are left bored and anxious. The argument over who is "right" ends without agreement, the bar closes, we run out of money at the casino, or we get tired from rushing around. Either way, once the drama ends, a mental and sometimes physical crash is inevitable. A high level of excitement is not a sustainable state.

Also, excitement tends to be relative to our expectations, so doing the same amount of rushing around, drinking, or gambling eventually becomes less stimulating. Since we naturally acclimate to a certain level of activity, we need to do more and more of it to keep it exciting. This, of course, can lead to a vicious cycle of ever-increasing periods of rushing around and frenetic activity, larger quantities of alcohol consumed, and more costly gambling junkets. This progression of excitement usually ends in suffering and misery.

The boredom that follows an exciting activity leads to a craving for the next excitement "high." Craving, as we have discovered, causes us to desire the future and be dissatisfied with the present. Desiring what does not exist inevitably makes us unhappy with the present, unhappy with that which is.

> " In general, all this excitement we Type As pursue causes our mental state to be constantly agitated, roiled up, and unstable. It is a roller coaster ride of emotions that causes suffering. "

In general, all this excitement we Type As pursue causes our mental state to be constantly agitated, roiled up, and unstable. It is a roller coaster ride of emotions that causes suffering. Excitement, as it turns out, is not the most pleasant of mental conditions to experience.

Peace, the alternative to excitement

The natural alternative to excitement is peace. Before you protest, peace is far more than just the lack of excitement; it is the presence of stillness, calm, and pleasant awareness of the present.

Because Type As have spent their lives pursuing excitement, peacefulness can be quite a foreign feeling, so unfamiliar that we may not have even considered it a possibility.

Excitement is not sustainable, but peace can be experienced and enjoyed for however long you desire. There is no need for an endpoint or "crash," emotional or physical.

Peace is a subject that has been explored, dissected, and discussed for thousands of years, and it is a centerpiece among Christian principles. Many of you may have noticed that my discussion of excitement also somewhat reflects Buddhist teachings. In fact, most or all world religions recognize peace as a key to godliness and happiness.

In retirement, chasing excitement is particularly useless and unnecessary. You no longer have to get ahead at work or impress others. You have the luxury of choosing your goals, which can be as few and as simple as you desire. In such an environment, what is the attraction of all of the rushing around and mental consternation? Why choose activities like abusing alcohol or gambling, which only lead to suffering and craving?

The allure of excitement will always be there for us Type As, and we will often fall prey to it. But give peace a chance. All of those wise people who have promoted this simple idea over the centuries were on to something.

CONTROLLING YOUR SPOUSE AND YOUR HOUSE: BEWARE

The weaker partner in a marriage is the one who loves the most.

—Eleanora Duse

This final chapter on expanding your personality to embrace attitudes and behaviors that do not come naturally to Type As addresses the potentially harmful effects of applying the controlling side of your personality to the first things you encounter on your first day of retirement: your awaiting spouse (if you have one) and your new daily venue, your house.

Many Type As exercise authority over other people during their careers. And even if they don't, they are very much in control of their work: they take it seriously, manage it tightly, and are extremely thorough. This is just how we Type As are built.

As a result, Type As may wake up at home on the first day of retirement and assume full command and control of their spouse and their household. It seems the natural, necessary, and useful thing to do. With no other outlet, they train their boundless energy and finely tuned leadership skills on their hapless spouse and the running of the household. Unfortunately for the spouse,

the sorts of questions Type As ask and statements they make are
something like this:

- Aren't you ever going to get out of bed?
- What are *we* going to do today?
- Why are you doing *that?*
- *We* need to clean out and organize the basement.
- Are you ever going to pay this bill?
- Just let me do it, so it gets done right!
- Is that all you are going to do all day?

I've observed that many freshly retired Type As fall into this
trap. It doesn't go well.

It isn't so much that retired Type As are inclined to tag along
with the spouse everywhere, which also would be annoying. Since
we are independent, that is less likely to be the problem. It is more
a matter of trying to control everything we see and experience,
and in retirement, our new purview is our spouse and household.

All of this monitoring, evaluating, and judging of our new daily
environment is not useful. It only causes both of you to suffer. You
cannot meaningfully control your spouse. At work, you had some
level of real influence and control of employees who reported to
you, and your spouse is (or certainly should be) a different case.
A good marriage is a partnership, not a dictatorship. If you were
to succeed in controlling your spouse, your spouse would not be
fully living his or her life, and neither would you. As in the quote
that opened this chapter, be the *loving one* if you are able. Since
assuming the weaker role simply isn't feasible for most Type
As, then you might at least recognize and appreciate how much

selflessness, compassion, and love it takes for your spouse to so often fill the subservient role in your relationship.

As a Type A, you are likely a logical person, so look at it this way: Attempting to control your spouse is bound to be a waste of your valuable time and effort. Why expend your energy on something so useless and certain to fail, and make both of you unhappy in the process? As an example, you cannot force your spouse to exercise more or to lose weight. It just might not be in the cards for them. Their body type and personality will ultimately prevail. So, focus on yourself, instead. Certainly, *you* could be in better shape or try a new form of exercise or a new sport. Do that, and leave your spouse to happily pursue his or her own path with more contentment.

> " Why expend your energy on something so useless and certain to fail, and make both of you unhappy in the process? "

In terms of controlling your household, let me put it bluntly: I don't know what you controlled at work, but over-managing and too tightly controlling your simple little household is also a tremendous waste of your time and talents. Come on, you can do better than that! If you insist on applying your energy to your household, then do something truly useful: clean something! Clean a bathroom, vacuum a room, wash a load of clothes, or just empty out the dishwasher. I really mean this. Your spouse, whether it is your husband or your wife, will be overcome with joy at this unexpected turn of events. Many men, in particular, find this work "not their job," or somehow beneath them, but once you are retired, you should both share equally in household tasks, to be fair. And just cutting the grass once a week is not equal sharing.

If I have just angered some of you, so be it. I'm here to give you the truth, not a load of BS!

Even if you are wise and aware enough to refrain from trying to control your spouse and household in retirement, you will still face the difficult transition of meshing your new routine with that of your spouse. Just being home every day with her or him will be a major challenge. And it will be even more of a challenge if your spouse has already been retired for a while and has established a "set" routine—because you will be crashing the party. It's a good idea to be ready for and sensitive to this major adjustment.

So just remember, as Dr. Seuss might have remarked, "Controlling your spouse and your house makes you a louse!"

PRACTICAL RULES
FOR LIVING IN RETIREMENT

> There is a fountain of youth...your mind, your talents, the
> creativity you bring to your life and the...people you love.
> When you learn to tap this source, you will truly have
> defeated age.
>
> —Sophia Loren

PRACTICAL RULE #1:

CARE FOR AND BE KIND TO YOURSELF

Lend yourself to others, but give yourself to yourself.

—Michel de Montaigne

In order to expand your Type A personality as I have suggested, you will need specific methods for implementing change. In other words, when you wake up each morning and face a new day in retirement, what can you do differently? How will you change your behavior to live more fully and experience all of the joy that is available to you?

I will address these specifics as I detail five practical rules for expanding your personality to live better in retirement. These practical rules cover self-care, putting accomplishments into perspective, learning not to rush, enjoying open time, and finding happiness in daily life.

Later in this section, I discuss other practical issues for living better in retirement—money, status, alcohol, exercise, and travel—based on my experiences thus far in retirement.

Practical Rule #1 is about taking care of you and being kind to you. It may seem kind of obvious, but the concept is deceptive and easy for many Type As to miss.

Why are we so hard on ourselves?

We Type As are so focused on productivity, accomplishment, and the like that we can be blind to something at least as important—ourselves. In the process of pursuing goals, we tend to ignore our personal well-being. When we get sick, how many of us demand that we go to work, anyway? Is the work a more important priority than taking care of ourselves? When we are tired at the end of a long day, we may ignore this feeling so that we can finish a project or complete our to-do list. And when we are frustrated or sad, we are not inclined to "give into" these feelings. That would be weak, and we definitely are not weaklings!

We Type As can be quite unforgiving of ourselves. Our expectations of ourselves are invariably sky-high and inflexible, even when our expectations of others are more realistic and forgiving. For instance, let's say you run into an old acquaintance. Your friend, who has put on a couple of pounds since last time you met, mentions how disappointed he is about his weight. You tell him he looks good. "You look fine, really. I didn't even notice!" And you really mean it. You think he is being too hard on himself.

But if *you* should put on a couple of pounds as reflected on that much too objective scale every morning, you berate yourself for it. It is unacceptable. "How could I let this happen?" Your worth plummets. You feel out of control.

Consider also the example of a close friend who confides that she has been feeling a little depressed lately. Work has been stressful, and she is having some marital difficulties. She tells you it has been hard to focus on work and all her other responsibilities because she has been lethargic. Many Type As would advise a friend that such lethargic periods are normal and to be expected. "It's okay to let some things slip a little bit. What's the big deal? Don't be so hard on yourself. You're a good person, and you'll feel better in time." But do we give ourselves the same good advice? Do we give ourselves a pass? Usually not.

People in general, but especially Type As, are severe with themselves yet often likely to cut others a break. The point is: why don't we treat ourselves with the same kindness and caring that we would offer a good friend? Why don't we qualify for our compassion? Why don't we love ourselves as much as we love others?

> " Why don't we treat ourselves with the same kindness and caring that we would offer a good friend? "

In retirement, you will have the extra time and opportunities to care for and be kind to yourself. You will no longer have an excuse not to do so.

How do I take care of and be kind to myself?

Both involve listening to your feelings and accepting your mood. If you are a little depressed one day, even for no specific reason, it is okay; it is acceptable. Life has its ups and downs. Difficult times help to define the good times, by contrast. Feel and explore the sadness a bit. You actually minimize the impact when you don't fight it; you will be treating your mind and body with care, compassion, and acceptance.

Take time to rest and relax. Let your mind and body regenerate and heal.

Your pets can serve as great examples of how to listen to your body and use common sense to guide your actions. I took my small dog out for a walk one very hot day, and I overextended him. Suddenly, he just plopped down on the ground. I kept pulling his leash to try to get him to start walking again, but he would have none of it. He was done. I had to carry the little fella home.

Good for him.

We should be so intuitive. In retirement, a good nap in the middle of a tiring day is the equivalent of being unwilling to walk anymore in the heat!

Of course, proper nutrition and exercise are fine ways to care for yourself. If you feel healthy, you will be happier.

Consider practicing acts of self-care and self-nurturing daily. By this, I mean doing things each day that you enjoy, things that have no productive purpose other than making you joyful. Do you enjoy going for a walk? Going out for ice cream? Getting a massage? Do it. And while doing such things, take your time and fully experience them. Other ideas include staying up late to watch a movie, skipping your morning exercise and going out for breakfast, or calling a good friend and chatting for a while. The list is infinite. The key is to simply indulge yourself every now and then: you are worth it, and the world won't stop spinning just because you aren't producing something for a little while.

One day, I sat down and made a list of things I enjoy for no reason except that I simply enjoy doing them, things that have no productive element. I listed almost a hundred different possibilities! Now, when I want to do something to care for myself, I just pick an item off the list and do it. We Type As love lists, and this can be your "fun" list!

Now, I know that some of you might consider this whole idea of focusing on yourself to be too selfish, something that will lead to the wrong priorities and unhappiness. You might contend that being more concerned with others is wiser and is the road to true happiness. I agree with you—except that you cannot be fully available and helpful to others unless you are healthy and well yourself. You need to take care of yourself—your body, your mind, and your essential needs—so that you will have energy and a positive attitude to be of excellent service to others. If not, you will slowly but surely lose energy, effectiveness, and joy, and then you will not be able to help very much. I agree that helping and serving others is the ultimate goal and the way to obtain true satisfaction and happiness, but you must take care of yourself first. Self-care does not have to demand the lion's share of your time, but it needs to be a priority.

Take care of and be kind to yourself every day, and you will be happier, more relaxed, and better able to serve others and pursue your retirement goals.

PRACTICAL RULE #2:

YOU ARE NOT YOUR ACCOMPLISHMENTS: WHY?

The Lord's blessing is our greatest wealth. All our work adds nothing to it!
—Proverbs 11:22

The second rule might seem odd at first, but once you explore it and see the truth in it, it is extremely powerful. Understanding that you are not your accomplishments can form the mental and emotional basis for being able to *allow* yourself to relax. It gives you an intellectual and emotional "get out of jail free card" when you feel burdened.

We Type As are prone to seeing ourselves as the sum total of what we have accomplished. This is true when we look back over our lives, or even when we review the day just past. We are what we produce!

This is not all bad. Being useful and productive is good. We, our families, and society benefit from our accomplishments. Yet, in retirement—with full-time work ended and our children, if any, raised—there is much less need for all this productivity.

However, let's dig down into the fundamental issue: why do we identify so strongly with what we have achieved? Is it really who we are? Are we completely lacking identity and self-worth without our accomplishments? Would the absence of accomplishments make us mere shells?

No, in fact, we are fully worthy—without *any* of our accomplishments.

We are worthy just by *being*.

You are worthy because you are *you*. You exist in, and are unique to, the universe. You have a soul. People love you, and you love others.

If you have a spouse who truly cares for you, they would love you just as much if you did less and had less. They love you, not your accomplishments. They may certainly appreciate and value your achievements, but you are fully loved regardless of them.

Not sure?

Don't you love your friends who are not as ambitious and have fewer achievements as much as you love those who are more successful? The less ambitious among them are still kind and caring souls—are they not as deserving of your friendship and love? Do you mete out your love based on the level of accomplishment? I doubt it. You treasure your friends for whom and what they are, considering them all equally special. Likewise, you are just as worthy of love from your friends, even without your merits and achievements.

> "You are worthy because you are *you*. You exist in, and are unique to, the universe. You have a soul."

You are also special because God made you.

He just enjoys watching you being you: Living your life, fumbling about, finding your way through this brief existence. He is fascinated by and loves you for all that you are: frustrated, ecstatic, busy, relaxed, focused, or just existing. All of it and any of it. He knows you are special because He made you.

God definitely loves you regardless of your accomplishments.

Shouldn't I be proud of my accomplishments?

Look back at the quote that opens this chapter. Accomplishments, or "good works" as they are often referred to in the Bible, are not so important to God. Something exists that is infinitely more important to Him, and it is the most significant thing we can offer: faith. God simply wants us to believe in Him.

As a hardcore Type A, I struggled mightily with this biblical concept. I understood the significance of faith, but I could never really understand why good works were so much less important to God. Aren't the things we *do* in this life, especially things like being kind and helpful to others, of utmost importance?

And while we're on the subject, I always wondered why pride is considered such a terrible sin. I never understood that, either. Shouldn't we be proud of ourselves and our accomplishments?

I have to admit that the Bible's lack of emphasis on good works and its disdain for pride always seemed counterintuitive to me—or just plain wrong. I think I have finally figured out why God views it this way. Bear in mind, I'm not a theologian, but I think I get this.

Faith is important to God because He wants us to show that we are willing to believe in Him despite any concrete proof: seeing, hearing, touching, and so forth. This is likely where the saying "leap of faith" comes from. It is supposed to be, indeed, a "leap" across the chasm, not made based on any hard evidence but solely on belief. We must know Him and love Him with all our hearts. He wants us to rely on Him, and Him alone, to guide and protect us through life. This is what God values most.

In fact, the only way to get to heaven is through faith, and faith alone. As the Bible states, "Then what can we boast about doing, to earn our salvation? Nothing at all. Because our acquittal is not based on our good deeds; it is based on what Christ has done and our faith in Him." (Romans 3:27)

It is worth noting that God still values our "good works" because He wants us to use our God-given talents while we are here, and not waste them. As Rick Warren states in his excellent book, *The Purpose Driven Life*: "You're not saved *by* service, but you are saved *for* service" (p. 228).

Now, what about pride? Pride is reviled in the Bible because it shows a lack of understanding and appreciation of *how we became* who and what we are.

Are you proud of how intelligent you are? Well, sorry to burst your bubble, but God gave you your high IQ. Proud of your career? God gave you the intelligence, energy, and work ethic, along with opportunities to pursue and excel at. Proud of the kids? God gave those to you, along with whatever energy, common sense, and patience you used in raising them. Are you getting the idea?

If you are proud, you display a fundamental misunderstanding of how you became what you are, and how you were able to create what you did while here on earth, which upsets Him. All glory must go to God.

When I mentioned at the outset of this chapter that Practical Rule #2 provides a sort of "get out of jail free card," what I meant is that the importance God places on faith versus good works means that you don't need to place so much emphasis on completing so many projects and tasks. God does not require this of you. Also, He will absolve all of your mistakes and sins. All you need to do is have faith in Him.

I don't know about you, but for me, this idea gave me huge relief. I could finally let go of so much that was burdening me. Whew!

Type A challenges and the "Why?" test

In Practical Rule #2, what do I mean when I say that you should ask "Why?"

Asking why is a means of determining what is actually worthy of your time, energy, and effort and what is not. Type As often do things just because they are a challenge, and not necessarily because they will result in any significant value. Sometimes, a goal is just the next mountain to climb.

Doing things solely for the challenge or just because you want to stay busy or prove something to someone else or yourself means you are wasting time on less than useful activities. Here are some examples to bring this concept to life for you.

After I was retired for a year or so, I became a bit bored, so I began searching for more challenge. Since I am a physical fitness buff, I considered taking on the demanding physical test of running a marathon. As I thought about why I should do it, however, the idea lost some of its luster. First, I learned that some physicians don't recommend training for and running a full marathon because such a long run can be extremely hard on your joints and on your body in general. Since I have problems with my lower back due to an injury suffered in my youth, my health would have been particularly vulnerable to the rigors of marathon training. But there was an even more important reason not to do a marathon: while I've done some running for exercise in the past, I never really liked it! I have always much preferred going to the gym and lifting weights.

So, why would I choose to run a marathon? Yes, it's challenging, and it certainly would add to my list of impressive accomplishments. But would it truly be worth it?

No. It didn't pass the "Why?" test. I couldn't determine why I would want to do it. Other types of activities or challenges would benefit me more and make me happier.

It's kind of odd, and I'm not sure it is entirely true, but sometimes it seems that we Type As torture ourselves for no apparent reason. We take on challenges that cause us physical and/or emotional pain, occasionally without justification. When I am in the gym lifting weights, sometimes I wonder about what I am doing: is weightlifting really for my good health, or am I just torturing myself? I don't know. But it is a valid question.

> " It didn't pass the 'Why?' test. I couldn't determine why I would want to do it. "

In retirement, with its myriad options and opportunities, it makes absolutely no sense to saddle ourselves with projects and activities from which neither we nor anyone else will derive much benefit. In fact, why do we need to have so many challenges, even if they are beneficial in some way? As I've said, God doesn't require it of us, and our families and good friends don't care, so why shouldn't we just relax and enjoy ourselves more?

What other challenges do Type As take on in retirement that may not pass the "Why?" test? Some examples are: starting a business, getting another degree, learning a foreign language, moving to upgrade or downsize our houses, or traveling across Europe. While any of these would make perfect sense for some of us, many Type As would undertake them for the wrong reasons: to have a new challenge just for challenge's sake, to busy ourselves and relieve our anxiety, or to needlessly prove something to others or ourselves.

You can also ask "Why?" to validate smaller tasks. Say I'm cutting the grass: I always edge it before I mow, but I hate edging because it is tedious. Rather than edging it every time I mow, why not edge it every other time? Who's going to notice? What's the difference?

I really believe that regularly asking "Why?" is an important key to helping Type As relax. Give yourself mental permission to pass on certain activities, and you will find it much easier to give in to relaxation.

I'll close this discussion with a Bible passage, which I think you'll find relevant:

> "As Jesus and the disciples continued on their way
> to Jerusalem they came to a village where a woman

named Martha welcomed them into her home. Her sister Mary sat on the floor, listening to Jesus as he talked.

"But Martha was the jittery type, and was worrying over the big dinner she was preparing.

"She came to Jesus and said, 'Sir, doesn't it seem unfair to you that my sister just sits here while I do all the work? Tell her to come and help me.

"But the Lord said to her, 'Martha, dear friend, you are so upset over all these details! There is really only one thing worth being concerned about. Mary has discovered it—and I won't take it away from her!'"

(Luke 10: 38–42)

When Jesus states that Mary has discovered "it," I believe he is referring to knowing, loving, and learning from God. Is preparing a meal, and being preoccupied with and focusing on all of the details associated with it, nearly as important as this? Or, in more general terms, are *any* of your daily tasks as essential as spending time with those who are important in your life, whether that is God, family, or friends?

PRACTICAL RULE #3:
THERE'S NEVER A GOOD REASON TO RUSH

A relaxed attitude lengthens a man's life.

—Proverbs 14:30

I have applied this rule repeatedly during my nine years in retirement, and I haven't yet found an exception to it.

Type As love to be in a hurry. Maybe it has to do with how much we enjoy the sense of accomplishment, or maybe it's because being in a hurry distracts us from uncomfortable emotions. Whatever the cause, rushing around is a constant companion. What I have discovered, however, is that being in a rush is never really useful.

For instance, you rush your spouse to get ready faster so you can leave to go to dinner at your friends' house. "We need to be there on time!" you admonish. Your spouse resents your pressure and attempt to control her as you hover, pacing back and forth. And what is the result? Either you get to your friends' house too early and have to kill time by driving around their neighborhood, or you arrive right on time. Either way, when you ring their doorbell precisely at the appointed time, you invariably catch them in a flurry of final preparations, which your hosts do not

> " Type As love to be in a hurry. Maybe it has to do with how much we enjoy the sense of accomplishment, or maybe it's because being in a hurry distracts us from uncomfortable emotions. "

appreciate. You stand there awkwardly as all the other guests arrive within the next half hour or so.

It sure was a good idea to rush your spouse to get there on time, huh?

In retirement, you will find that you have plenty of time to perform your daily tasks and have no need to rush. Yet, somehow, the allure of rushing around often rears its ugly head.

Here is an example from my own experience. It occurred early on in my retirement. I was doing some errands on a weekday morning. I had only a couple of stops to make and plenty of time to complete them. In fact, I had nothing planned for the remainder of the day. So, what happened? As I was driving to my last stop, still well before noon, I got pulled over for speeding. I was going 62 in a 45-mph zone!

Even I couldn't miss the irony in that.

Was there nothing worth listening to on the radio while I was driving? Was there no scenery worth appreciating or some idle thoughts worth entertaining? How about just relaxing and being calm?

How did I feel as I was rushing along? I felt stressed. And to what end? Even if I hadn't gotten nabbed for speeding, completing my tasks so quickly would only get me home that much sooner, potentially sentenced to boredom once I arrived.

As a Type A, you will probably always have the desire to rush around, but it simply makes sense to resist the impulse.

A good test

Let's take the "never rush" rule to its logical extreme and see what the result is.

Let's say you are walking through the mall when, suddenly, you are confronted with the medical emergency of a stranger. Since he is an older person, he might be having a heart attack, a stroke, or worse. Whatever it is, it appears quite serious. He is crumpled up on the ground, gasping for breath. He needs help, now!

This is a time to rush if there ever was one, right?

Well, actually, no. Medical professionals tell us that we need to keep a level head in such a situation and do certain things strictly in order of priority; this will give the person the best chance of survival. For instance, it is usually best to contact medical help, such as calling 911 on your cell phone, before rendering any assistance so that medical professionals can arrive on the scene as quickly as possible. Then, you might try to find an AED device (automated external defibrillator) or a security guard who might have some medical training or at least know what else to do. Rushing might cause you to make mistakes, which could prove fatal for the hapless stranger.

You are *always* best served by taking your time with tasks and activities instead of rushing to complete them, which serves no useful purpose. In so doing, you will be more productive, not less, and you will get the additional benefit of deriving much more enjoyment and satisfaction from your activities.

How about a day of rest?

Even when I have repeatedly fallen into the trap of rushing around during the week, which still happens to me regularly, I have found that I can salvage some restfulness and peace if I choose to use Sunday as a day only for rest and contemplation, and nothing else. This practice has proved to be quite beneficial for a stubbornly habitual Type A like me. It is easy to get caught up in the flow of normal daily activities during the week and rush around, but I find that I can cure some of those ills by honoring Sunday as a day of rest. If you commit to a lack of "doing," productivity, and accomplishment on Sundays, if you lay all tasks aside for even that one day a week, you will at least create a small island of peace in your week.

You might also choose to rest on Sundays for the additional reason that the Bible tells us to do so. I find that some quiet time on Sundays gives God a few minutes to "speak" to me without the clutter and noise of my daily business interfering and crowding it out.

Interestingly, setting aside Sundays for rest carries with it another benefit that I have touched on earlier. It "proves" to you that you can stop for a while. It confirms that you are able to manage your activity level and not be a slave to it. The idea of being a slave to your activities might seem kind of strange because, of course, we can choose what we do and don't do, right? In fact, though, Type As can get stuck on a treadmill of activity and accomplishment, and then we fear

> "
> Setting aside Sundays for rest 'proves' to you that you can stop for a while."

stepping off it. It feels like we might lose control over our lives if we do. Carving out Sunday, or some other day of the week, as a day of peace and inactivity proves to us that our lives and the world will not fall apart if we stop and relax for a little while.

PRACTICAL RULE #4:

SEEK OUT AND ENJOY OPEN TIME

Boredom is the feeling that everything is a waste of time;
serenity, that nothing is.

—Thomas Szasz

For all of your adult life, your responsibilities have kept you tied
to a schedule. Retirement provides an excellent opportunity to get
free. You have been very productive—good for you. Now, though,
is a great time to take a break. Revel in unscheduled or "open"
time. Get bored. Find new things to do. Do what you want, all day,
every day!

I'm going to predict that if you stop your constant scheduling
and activity for a few moments and it happens that you become
a little bit bored, you probably won't die.

Many Type As fear retirement because they are afraid of
open time. They are afraid they won't know what to do with
themselves. Remember, earlier in the book, I gave you the key
to being able to relax and enjoy open time: Simply sit with your
emotions and feelings and experience them, and you will be able
to find your core of calm and peace.

Now, I am asking you to consider more than occasional, unexpected moments of unscheduled time. I'm asking you to consciously and actively seek out longer periods of unscheduled time and to do it regularly. These can be islands of tranquility and joy in your retirement experience.

I intentionally leave large, almost glaring, gaps in my schedule these days. I no longer feel anxious about them because I have learned something: unscheduled time is not only good for me, but it is also fun. Let's say I have exercise planned for first thing in the morning, then a couple of errands, and afterward I will have lunch. For the afternoon, I might have nothing in particular planned. This leaves me a nice patch of open time that day.

What I do with unstructured time

What might I actually do on such afternoons? Sometimes I am just tired for some reason; maybe I did a hard workout that day or had a lousy sleep the night before. What leaps to mind in this instance? I'll take a nice nap! If I'm only a little weary, I might just lie on the couch in the family room. But if I'm tired, I take my clothes off and take a power nap in my bedroom.

I've become king of the "no-regrets nap" these days!

Sometimes, since my wife and I both enjoy it, we go to a movie in the afternoon. Weekday afternoons are a great time to go to the movies. It's not crowded, so you can get there any time prior to show time and get a great seat.

Sometimes, I just flick on the TV and look for an interesting program. I can't watch that tabloid-type daytime reality TV, though, maybe because I truly dislike it, or maybe because I'm afraid I might like it too much and start watching it every day!

One of my favorite unstructured activities is to go to the pet store and see the puppies. The only problem with this is that I want to take all the little fellas home.

You get the point. The idea is to allow yourself to unwind, to "unbusy" your mind and body, and allow yourself to explore and experience life in its simplest form.

Why Type As are uncomfortable with open time

You might still be skeptical. If you are, it could be that you are still somewhat unconvinced that handling open time can be so easy. The idea of big holes in your schedule throughout the week may make you uncomfortable, and if that's the case, I don't blame you. It was very difficult for me to become at ease with it. In fact, it took me years to fully embrace it. It may be equally hard for you, after decades of being so scheduled, to learn how to enjoy leaving your life so open.

Those of you who struggle with relaxing, as I did, might need more guidance than I have provided thus far. I have found that sitting with my emotions and accepting them is a highly effective means of learning how to relax. Beyond that, I have two additional perspectives I think you might consider. I have discussed them before, but I want to emphasize them and be quite specific.

At its root, being uneasy about open time is based on two key misconceptions.

> " The idea is to allow yourself to unwind, to 'unbusy' your mind and body, and allow yourself to explore and experience life in its simplest form. "

Guilt about not being productive

Most Type As feel guilty about relaxing. During my struggles with relaxation, I realized that I felt guilty about doing nothing and being unproductive. This is because we Type As derive so much of our self-worth and self-esteem from doing and achieving. There is no reason to feel guilty about spending time on you. Your family and friends do not require constant productivity and activity from you. More important, God does not require this from you, either. You can feel good about all of your accomplishments thus far in life. Be content with what you have achieved and enjoy this last phase of your life. Choose to let go of the guilt.

Fear of feeling out of control

There is a second misconception we Type As labor under. We often experience anxiousness, dread, or outright fear at the prospect of unscheduled time. It's that idea that you won't know what to do with yourself and will feel out of control, which is especially frightening to Type As. However, there is no justification for it. As I have said about relaxation, you can handle your emotions and enjoy open time. There is no reason to be scared.

So, if you likewise sense the twin emotions of guilt and fear when considering the open time represented by the prospect of retirement, or simply leaving unscheduled time or a gap in your day, realize that neither is justified. Expose these emotions to the light of day and see them for what they really are, which is a falsehood, a wisp.

PRACTICAL RULE #5:

FIND SOME JOY EACH DAY

The time to be happy is now. The place to be happy is here.

—Robert Green Ingersoll

The last practical rule for living well in retirement is closely related to seeking out and enjoying open time: finding joy in your life, each and every day.

As achievement-seeking Type As, it seems we are constantly working to get ahead, and this can become particularly single-minded during our careers. When we are in this mode, we are deferring gratification. We tell ourselves that we are denying ourselves pleasure for good reason. We are building a *future*. This mythic future will be an "ideal state," at which point we will be wonderfully happy. If asked whether we are enjoying ourselves, we would say no, but it's all part of our brilliant plan!

As you might have guessed, the problem is that we become so accustomed to working constantly and deferring gratification that we may never stop, even after we retire, because it has become such an ingrained habit. If, in fact, we never stop, then what we were building never materializes. The Promised Land of this future state never arrives. This is the life that ends on a workday morning when your spouse finds you face-down in your cornflakes, remember?

Deferring gratification implicitly assumes that we can predict with some certainty how long we will live, or simply maintain our health, so that we can eventually enjoy what we have built. At what specific point do we finally stop deferring our enjoyment and begin allowing ourselves to immerse ourselves in it? When the kids all graduate from college? When we retire? When we are sixty-five? Seventy? Unfortunately, the Big Guy upstairs is the only one who knows when we will lose our good health or die. We all know people in their forties and fifties who were befallen by some unexpected health issue like cancer, stroke, heart attack, Parkinson's, rheumatoid arthritis, major back/hip/knee problems, a car accident, or the like, and who were never the same or passed away as a result.

> " We are building a **future**. This mythic future will be an 'ideal state,' at which point we will be wonderfully happy. If asked whether we are enjoying ourselves, we would say no, but it's all part of our brilliant plan! "

If retirement isn't the time to begin enjoying life, then when is?

A very simple and effective way to start savoring life for its own merits is to choose at least one joyful thing to do every day. You can choose an activity from your list of self-care and self-nurturing activities. This is a great way to experience a few moments of joyful living.

Let's say you are immersed in some project, such as a home improvement. It is a worthwhile endeavor, and you are very focused on it. This is fine, but remember to find the joy. There is no reason to torture yourself with your project. You can work on it for a few hours and then, say, go and get yourself an ice cream. Or you can take a little break to read an interesting book you haven't gotten to for a while. The project you are working on isn't going anywhere. When you get back to it, it will be as you left it, no better or worse. And you just might bring a little more energy and an improved perspective with you when you return to it.

I volunteer three days a week at a local hospital. Because I am such a Type A, I tend to be very busy and productive while I am there. This is good and helpful, but I find that I often spend most of my time at the hospital with my head down, absorbed in what I'm doing, and thereby miss some of the joy I might have gained.

Early on in my volunteering career, a nurse told me, "Tim, we get the benefit of your work, and that is great, but we want to get to know *you*. We don't get the benefit of spending time with you!"

What a nice and kind remark, and what a revelation to me at the time. My co-workers don't just value me as a worker and producer; they value me as a *person*. Also, as part of their own work lives, they not only want to do a good job, but they also want to enjoy the experience. What a concept!

From that experience and others, I have come to realize that my time spent at the hospital can be more pleasant, and often even more useful, if I take some time during my shift to just relax and chat with the doctors, nurses, and staff. No one cares that I take a little time to recharge my batteries and be sociable.

And the hospital will certainly not grind to a halt because of my brief inactivity. In fact, taking time out at the hospital to enjoy the company of my co-workers is a win-win situation. We all benefit, and nothing is lost.

Now, we will explore five other practical issues that present themselves in retirement.

THE ISSUE OF MONEY

> There are necessary evils. Money is an important thing in terms of representing freedom in our world.
>
> —Johnny Depp

Staying retired is important to anyone who has decided to retire. Choosing to work for the joy of it is one thing, but having to work because you need the money to live is quite another. This is why the issue of money in retirement is worthy of some attention.

Countless books have been written on the subject of how much money you need to accumulate for a comfortable retirement, so I will not address that question. However, I want to explore the topic of spending in retirement based on some interesting experiences I've had while retired and a few conclusions I have reached as a result.

When I first retired, I'll admit, I went on a bit of a spending spree. This is common for Type As. The "excitement" of work, whether it is positive or negative, needs to be replaced with something, and enjoyable spending projects can fit the bill. I know that very conservative Type As are quite controlled in their spending habits and would not allow themselves to fall prey to this inclination, but many of us will not be able to resist the allure.

Many new retirees train their initial focus on their homes, since that is where they will be spending much of their time. Career-driven Type As were so busy at work that a lot of deferred maintenance built up in their houses. These projects gnawed at us, but we just didn't have enough time and didn't make it enough of a priority to address them. Now, we have nothing but time, so we can finally clean up the "mess." Creating a sense of order in our environment is satisfying.

As a bona fide Type A, I was no exception. First thing in retirement, I created a list of all of the repairs that needed to be done to our house and got to work. That seems harmless enough, right?

Well, as I was working on these minor repairs, my wife and I decided we could also use some significant home improvements. (Actually, she decided this, and I wisely fell in line.) We decided to remodel our master bath, which turned out quite nicely. In fact, the final bill reflected just how nice it was.

Human behavior being what it is, one thing led to another. We began making some improvements to our yard. First, we put in a pond. We enjoyed the pond so much that we decided to remove our aboveground pool and replace it with a garden; with our kids grown and out of the house, we weren't using it much. What a fun idea!

> " Human behavior being what it is, one thing led to another. "

Unchecked, you can see where this could be headed: back to work to make more money. I decided these spending projects were not nearly enough fun to force me back into the workforce.

As I pondered these early retirement experiences and thought about the role of money in retirement, I came to some conclusions. I determined it would be useful to categorize retirement activities related to money into three types: earning, spending, and free. Earning activities are those that produce some income, like a part-time job. Spending activities are those that involve the outflow of money, such as the home improvement projects we had undertaken. Last, free activities are those that neither produce income nor incur expense, such as volunteering, and therefore they are neutral relative to money.

Such categorization is important and instructive because, as you are pursuing your passions and using the trial-and-error method of selecting projects, you need to be aware of the financial impact of your choices. While this might seem obvious, it is easy to start down a road of spending in retirement that seems innocuous enough at the outset but then leads to financial problems.

In my situation, the flurry of spending had indeed arrived at a reckoning point. Yes, it was fun. Much of our spending might even have been a reasonably worthwhile investment in our property. Regardless, it had to stop or it would jeopardize our financial situation. And that was unacceptable. Of all the things my wife and I enjoyed about retirement, our independence from the world of full-time work was the most satisfying and had the greatest value.

Home improvements are just one example of how well-intentioned activities in retirement can get out of hand financially. The same can happen with new hobbies, some of which can become black holes of spending if you're not careful.

Spending activities

Let's explore spending activities in retirement a bit further by breaking them down into a finer level of detail. First, consider that spending activities can be classified as either one-time or recurring. An example of one-time spending is a charitable gift to an organization. This expenditure can be "one and done" if you so choose (and if the charitable organization doesn't harass and shame you into contributing again the following year!). A single vacation trip is also a one-time expense.

A longer-term plan, such as developing an intention to travel to several international destinations over a period of years, is somewhat more hazardous to your financial health; it involves a plan to spend quite a bit of money over time, but at least you can stop this series of trips at any point you choose. It is a recurring expenditure, but not the most risky type.

More financially perilous would be the decision to move to a more expensive home. It is unlikely that you would choose to move to a bigger house in retirement, but you might decide to move from, say, a suburban house to a swanky condo downtown. This expenditure is potentially more problematic than the international travel itinerary because it involves recurring expenses, like increased property taxes and maintenance, which you cannot discontinue easily. The only way to reduce them would be to make the difficult decision of selling the new home and moving to something cheaper, which would be painful and disruptive. In retirement, you must choose higher recurring expenses such as these very carefully.

Earning activities

From my three categories of activities in retirement, the least financially precarious ones are of course earning and free activities. Besides a full- or part-time job, earning activities include hobbies that produce income. Some people have a talent for and enjoy creating paintings, sculptures, arts-and-crafts, or refurbishing furniture, and the like. If you can make some money at something you enjoy, all the better.

Free activities

Along with volunteering, many hobbies fall into this category. Some hobbies are inexpensive, like woodcarving or cooking, but some are so expensive that they cannot be considered in this free category, such as collecting rare antiques. Most forms of exercise fall into the free-activity category, such as walking, running, and inexpensive gym memberships. Also, if you have developed a self-care and self-nurturing list, as I suggested in an earlier chapter, many of these activities are free. They include simple pleasures like spending time with your grandchildren, taking a relaxing bath, visiting a local museum, or going to a pet store to see the puppies and kittens. (Just don't fall in love with one and bring it home, which would become a recurring expenditure.) You can engage in activities like these to your heart's content without jeopardizing your finances.

Pure expenses and expenses with an investment component

Spending activities can be further broken down to those that are "pure expense" and those that have some investment component.

Pure expenses are things like vacations and even charitable gifts, in that the money spent is simply gone forever.

In contrast, purchasing a more expensive home, a classic car, or a valuable piece of art—and even certain types of home improvements—have at least some potential as investments. Since you will likely be able to sell these assets in the future, either with some appreciation in price or at least with only a small decline in value, you will get most or some of this money back later. I wouldn't, however, consider a non-classic car or motorcycle much of an investment; they depreciate so rapidly that they make very poor investments. Such items are purchased for consumption, so to speak.

Finally, by way of example, the most fiscally dangerous activity you could undertake in retirement, and I am only half kidding, would probably be buying a boat, or worse yet, a big boat. The initial purchase price is high, followed by the "joy" of substantial recurring expenditures, such as repairs and maintenance, gasoline, docking, storage, and so forth. And when it comes time to sell it, get ready for a nasty surprise: used boats don't fetch a high resale price. Perhaps this accounts for the saying that the two best days of boat ownership are the day you buy it and the day you sell it!

Even so, this doesn't mean that you should not buy a boat or any other so-called "poor investment" in retirement. If it will make you happy enough, it might very well be worth the cost. Just go into it with your eyes open and some sort of plan.

Before you plunge into buying some new, expensive toy, you might also want to consult with your spouse. I've heard that divorce is also quite expensive.

THE ISSUE OF STATUS

Those who humble themselves shall be exalted.

—Matthew 23:11

Retirement is a time of great change, not just financially, but also emotionally.

Most people derive their identity and self-worth largely from their jobs, rightly or wrongly. This seems to be especially true in America and especially true of Type As. We are what we do. Just meet a new acquaintance at a cocktail party and notice what the first question usually is: "So, what do you do for a living?"

When you retire, you lose most of your identification with your career. You are now a retiree, whatever that signifies, a retiree who *used to be* an engineer or teacher or police officer. Our culture does not confer much status upon retirees, or on older people in general.

Workers in the twilight of their careers, prior to retirement, are usually respected for the knowledge and skills they have developed over the years. Having worked diligently at their jobs for decades, they are valued and respected by their bosses, or if not, at least by their fellow workers, customers, and so forth. Their family and friends also view them as people who have contributed much to their companies, their families, and society. All of this confers a certain amount of status on the near-retiree.

Also, since Type As tend to be achievement-oriented, many rose to positions in their career that carry special markers of status. By this, I mean things like a fancy title, a lot of responsibility and power, many subordinates, high compensation, and special perks (bonuses, an office, an assistant). Every perk bestows even more respect and social status. Many get quite attached to these earmarks of success, which become part of their identity. If you are one of these fortunate few, once you retire, even if you still have a lot of money and have kept the big house and fancy car, no one anymore calls you "Mr." or "Ms." in a tone of deference (except maybe the neighborhood kids). You no longer wield power over a group of adoring (or so they seemed) minions. No one seeks out and bestows great value on your decision-making prowess. Your only title now is "retired person."

> " Since Type As tend to be achievement-oriented, many rose to positions in their career that carry special markers of status. "

Sudden loss of status

For all new retirees, regardless of the level they achieved within the company hierarchy, the sudden loss of status can come as quite a shock. Some handle it well—others, not so much.

In response to this loss, Type As often seek out status-bearing responsibilities in retirement to fill the gap and make them feel whole again.

In this regard, you have several options. You can become a part-time teacher or consultant, which carry some status. If you were at the highest levels within your company, a seat on a corporate board, either in your industry or with a non-profit organization like a hospital, might be available. This can be productive and a source of responsibility and distinction. Volunteer opportunities and part-time jobs with charitable organizations in supervisory or leadership capacities exist. These are prestigious positions in which you also can be helpful. Working as a fundraiser can provide a good opportunity to wield some power and make a difference. Heck, you might even be able to follow Bill Clinton around the globe and save the world!

There is an alternate path, however, that I would like to humbly (pun intended) suggest.

For some, this other path comes quite naturally. There are a couple of reasons for this. Either they were not among the "chosen few" who enjoyed a lot of special-status markers at work, or they had them and for some reason did not become particularly attached to them. The alternate road I am suggesting entails embracing *lack of status* as a conscious choice.

> " The alternate road I am suggesting entails embracing **lack of status** as a conscious choice. "

Help for the sake of helping and not for prestige

Why would you decide to "lower" yourself in this fashion? "After all," you might say, "I didn't gain all of this knowledge and develop all these managerial and leadership skills to simply abandon them upon retiring, when I could still use them productively. Wouldn't that be a sign of failure, or at the very least, a huge step backward?"

Well, if I may be so bold as to quote God on this one, the answer is a resounding "No!" It is *not* a step backward in your progression as a person. It can, in fact, be one of your greatest leaps forward.

I've discussed pride before, and that God dislikes it. God wants us to humble ourselves before others and before Him. Matthew 23:11 states: "The more lowly your service to others, the greater you are. To be the greatest, be a servant." God views humble service as the highest human calling.

You could respond to this by saying that many positions of status in retirement also involve admirable service, like the examples I gave of consulting, corporate board work, and fundraising. Yes, these are quite useful activities and still pleasing to God, and if you happen to enjoy being a leader, that does not make you a bad or shallow person. Many useful and godly pursuits you might get involved in add a lot of value to society while also conferring some status. You might even argue that you are "leveraging" your skills more fully by being in a position of more responsibility and therefore able to affect more people or generate more results.

By all means, do what makes sense for you. Be happy. And help the world in the process, if you are so inclined.

However, I have found that an important difference exists between taking on a status job and taking on a no-prestige role, like cleaning cages at a Humane Society facility or wiping down bloody surgical beds in a hospital.

The difference is that, in a role that lacks any status, you are helping just for the sake of helping. It strips the activity of all earthly reward—recognition, power, money, fame, and so forth. And, in my experience, when you help just for the sake of helping, you realize what life is all about. I have come to recognize that life is mostly about people helping each other through difficult and trying times. I believe that life is about knowing God and serving Him, without questioning why or what's in it for you. I think this is why God values lowly and humbling service so much.

I must say that the people you meet when you are helping at the lowest level in an organization are some of the kindest, sweetest, and most genuine people you could ever hope to meet. I'm not saying that management doesn't have its share of "good eggs," but I have to admit I kind of favor the worker bees. If you are in a position of power, the inclination is to breeze by these lower-level employees in a rush to your next meeting. You might even think, privately, how simple-minded and boring they must be.

Well, I work at a hospital, often right alongside the maintenance employees and housekeepers, and I love them. To a person, they are caring and sweet, and they are also smart, wise, and funny. And they know more about those "upper-level" types than you may think!

Are they perfect? Of course not. But they are honest and hardworking people, and they are worth meeting and spending some time with, I can guarantee you that.

Just give it a little thought. Both high-level and low-level jobs in retirement are useful and productive. But ask yourself: "Can I better myself more as a *person* by taking on a strictly servant role?" It is a question worth addressing for at least a moment.

ALCOHOL: A CAUTIONARY TALE

Alcohol...doesn't fill up anyone's psychological gaps, all it replaces is the lack of God. It doesn't comfort man. On the contrary...it transports him to the supreme regions where he is master of his own destiny.

—Marguerite Duras

I have always been a pretty hard drinker. It may be because I'm Irish or because, as a Type A, I have relied on alcohol to relax. For whatever reason, I have a long history of "partying it up."

I've had a lot of fun times while drinking with friends. Sprinkled in with the fun have also been some disasters. Anyone who drinks often has had some bad nights. You know what I mean because either you have experienced it personally or witnessed first-hand the train wreck of another "over-served" person at a bar or party.

With this as a backdrop, I entered retirement. I was very happy about my decision to retire and being able to do so at such a relatively young age and with solid finances. So, for the first few months, I whooped it up with the alcohol. It was one big party! And I enjoyed myself for the most part, despite a few reckless nights and some serious hangovers.

After that initial rush of excitement, I eventually settled back into my usual pattern of drinking only on Friday and Saturday nights. Not every Friday and Saturday, but most. I had several drinks when I did drink, but I kept it confined to the weekends.

A craving for excitement

After about a year into retirement, I got a little bored with my situation. I was looking for some excitement. I was enjoying my drinking on the weekends and always looked forward to it a great deal. So, I figured, why not drink more often? Hey, I was retired, so I could do whatever I wanted! As a good, card-carrying Type A, I was going to go for it.

It started out innocently enough. After a long, brutal day of running my two or three errands (I'm kidding, of course), I felt entitled to a few drinks on, say, a Tuesday evening. What a great idea!

Of course, if it was fun to have a drink or two or three on Tuesday night, why not again on Thursday night?

Within a couple of months of expanding my drinking to the weekday evenings, it dawned on me, in a flash of blinding revelation, why not have a glass of wine as I lay by the pool in the afternoon? (We live in a neighborhood with a community pool.) It might spice up those mundane situations in which I've run out of good reading material or there is no one to talk to. Brilliant!

I think you can see where this is headed.

The coup de grace, then, as inevitable as it was, occurred.

On this particular Saturday night, I was drinking at home with my wife, twenty-nine-year-old son, his girlfriend, and my father-in-law and mother-in-law. I was getting pretty stewed, yet I was still bored and unsatisfied. All of the drinking on the weekends, on weekday nights, and at the pool, rather than satisfying my craving for alcohol, only increased it to a fever pitch. In fact, it had turned me into an alcohol- and excitement-craving monster (often also referred to as an addict).

While sitting with that innocent, unsuspecting group of family, I suddenly stood up and announced that we should all go to a strip club! I told them that our party was too boring for me, and that we always do the same old thing. "Let's live a little!"

I had been to strip clubs on a couple of occasions. I had enjoyed myself, but it never seemed like a big deal. Those experiences, however, occurred with a group of male friends or co-workers. Now, with my judgment and thinking hijacked by copious amounts of alcohol, I was insisting that we go to one of these clubs with my son, his girlfriend, and my mother-in-law in tow!

Looking back now, I see that my stupidity was breathtaking.

Well, to my surprise—and to the credit of the group I was with for being so accommodating and flexible—after much pleading by me, they relented and said they would go.

> " It dawned on me, in a flash of blinding revelation, why not have a glass of wine as I lay by the pool in the afternoon? "

Fearing they might change their minds, I immediately called for a cab to transport us to the "Promised Land."

I was already drunk when we arrived, and it was all-downhill from there. I attempted to order a bottle of champagne, and while the cocktail waitress thought this was an excellent idea, my wife was a bit less enthused and wisely nixed it.

Without going into all of the gory detail, our family's strip-club adventure was not what I had hoped it would be. The strip-club experience, I discovered, was diminished somewhat by the presence of such family members as my son, his girlfriend, and the in-laws. You think?

"The day after," as the story goes, was, well, the day after, with all its attendant and much deserved pain and suffering.

"What was that all about last night?" I pondered. "What the heck was I doing?"

For a few weeks, I stopped drinking entirely, understandably. Then, gradually, I began to drink again, but quite a bit more cautiously. I still had an occasional night of binge drinking, but nothing even remotely rivaling "the great strip-club adventure."

I didn't question my relationship with alcohol until a year or so later, when I started reading about Vipassana meditation and crystallizing my thoughts about excitement versus peace. You can imagine how this concept hit home. It described me on alcohol, exactly.

Looking back on my experiences with alcohol, I realized that I had begun the process by liking alcohol and becoming attached to it and its alluring effects. Soon, I started craving it, at first just occasionally, and then more and more. I became increasingly attached to it. When I didn't have it, I craved it, and simultaneously felt aversion to whatever I was doing at the moment, since it never measured up to the excitement of being on alcohol. I was averse to most or all of what I did during the week, because whatever it was, it was not as much fun as drinking. So, when

I wasn't drinking, which of course was most of the time, I was also not in the present or enjoying the moment. This cycle, and all of its accompanying mental consternation, caused me much suffering and misery. It continued to intensify, as vicious cycles do, leading to the inevitable denouement. Excitement at these levels can never be sustained and must eventually fall to earth.

Does that about sum it up?

As I began thinking about excitement in general, I realized that, by my nature, I was an excitement junkie. Not in the "extreme sports" kind of way, like jumping out of a plane, but in the way of always wanting mental excitement to occupy my mind, make me feel energized and in control, and keep me continually busy. It was dawning on me how futile this was, and I began to understand the unsustainable nature of it.

Finally, I was starting down the path to enlightenment.

During a visit to a therapist at around this same time, I relayed the alcohol experiences to her. After I finished my tale of woe, she had an interesting comment, something I hadn't considered. She said, "Tim, you are such a dedicated workout guy, and so health conscious in most of your lifestyle, I'm actually surprised that you even drink at all."

That was when it all gelled for me, at least relative to alcohol. She was right, of course. What was alcohol really doing for me? Why was I choosing to drink at all? Even small amounts of alcohol develop craving for it, especially in someone like me, since apparently I have a somewhat addictive personality. Also, I was often sick from being hung-over, which isn't very enjoyable. The whole thing was just a bad trip.

I decided to stop drinking entirely. For me, it was the best decision, and I have never regretted it. I found that alcohol was not adding anything positive to my life. I had drunk a lot during my working years, probably mostly because of the stress of my high-powered jobs and my not-yet-learned ability to relax without alcohol. Now that I was retired, truly loved my life, and had begun to learn how to relax, I discovered that alcohol had no benefit for me. In fact, the craving that it caused was a major source of suffering. I just didn't enjoy it at all anymore.

Do what makes sense for you

I am not relating this story because I want to climb up on some soapbox and convince you to give up alcohol. That is not my intention, and it probably doesn't even make sense for most of you. Many people seem to be able to manage alcohol in a way that does not cause them much suffering or get them into an inordinate amount of trouble. If this is the case with you, great.

On the other hand, there are some Type As like me who have such a go-for-it-all mentality that alcohol can present serious problems, and retirement is fertile ground for the development of alcohol abuse, what with the decrease in responsibility and the long, unscheduled stretches of time.

So, for those of you who have a tendency to abuse alcohol, I can tell you that I took the alcohol thing out pretty much as far as you can; I took it out to its logical limit. Now, I can report that nothing is there, nothing that is at all worth pursuing.

I have no illusion that my story will keep any of you from proceeding down the same rabbit hole I traveled. That's kind of how alcohol is: most people need to experience it for themselves.

At the very least, I hope you found my experience a good example of how the principles of Vipassana meditation and peace can be applied to troublesome areas of one's life. If not, hopefully you found it a bit amusing!

WHY EXERCISE IS EVEN MORE IMPORTANT THAN YOU THINK

Training [exercise] gives us an outlet for suppressed energies created by stress and thus tones the spirit just as [it] conditions the body.

—Arnold Schwarzenegger

I will go out on a limb here and say that Type As are more likely to be exercisers, and particularly avid exercisers, compared to the population as a whole. It's just our nature. Being ambitious, driven, controlling, and maybe just a bit vain, exercise is an activity we gravitate toward.

Unless you have been living in a hole for the past thirty years, you are likely aware that exercise is excellent for your health. As such, it definitely qualifies for your list of self-care activities. Done properly and consistently, exercise improves your cardio-respiratory system, muscle tone, strength, and flexibility, and helps ward off many ailments and diseases. Many in the medical community believe that lack of activity and obesity, rather than merely aging, causes most of the sickness experienced in late life. And here is a perk: Exercise is a great way to elevate your mood.

It releases chemicals in your body called endorphins that have a natural mood-elevating effect.

If you live in northern geographic regions, you may experience acute onset of mild to moderate depression during the cold and cloudy winter months. I know I do. This is called seasonal affective disorder (SAD), and it can be quite debilitating. SAD is caused by lack of sunlight and possibly the decreased activity level that is common during the winter months.

With their boundless energy, Type As are especially likely to feel cooped up and somewhat claustrophobic during the cold and dark winter months, when there is less opportunity for outside activity, which could exacerbate SAD symptoms. However, even if there is no direct correlation between Type A personality and seasonal affective disorder, if you feel any gloominess during the winter, you can benefit from the following advice.

In my experience, regular exercise during the winter months can do much to alleviate the winter blues. If you can bear to exercise outside when it is cold—walking, running, skiing, shoveling snow, for example—the exposure to natural light will provide an additional benefit. Exercising at your local gym under the bright indoor lights, while not nearly as therapeutic as exercising in the sunlight, can be restorative. Just being in the gym with a bunch of optimistic and active people in pursuit of improving themselves is a mood elevator of sorts.

In fact, exercise all year round is important for Type As, especially during retirement, because we need to find a consistent and productive means of burning off our excess energy so that we can slow down and relax. Exercise, or some other energy-burning activity, will assist you in implementing many of my other recommendations for retirement, such as pacing, taking time to rest, and enjoying open time. I'll explain why.

I don't know about you, but when I wake up in the morning, I'm raring to go. I simply could not enjoy spending the first hour of my day, say, sitting on the couch and reading the newspaper. I could try to force myself to do it, but it would feel completely unnatural and make me unhappy. I choose not to deny who I am in this instance, so even in retirement, I am always looking for something active to do first thing in the morning.

Even if you are not as much of a morning person as I am, at some point in the day, as a Type A, your motor starts to rev up. As I said, it's part of our nature. I have found that if I address this stored-up energy by engaging in a positive, energy-burning activity, the rest of my day is much more enjoyable.

Let's say I don't begin my day without first burning off some energy. If, instead, I try to read the newspaper first, I am likely to just skim through the headlines impatiently, finishing the newspaper in a couple of minutes, having comprehended little and certainly gaining no depth of understanding. Then, if I were to take the dog for a walk, I would likely drag the poor guy around the block by his leash in an effort to quickly get to my next activity. This is not much fun for the little fella—or me. Then I would likely dash off on my errands, rushing from stop

> " I have found that if I address this stored-up energy by engaging in a positive, energy-burning activity, the rest of my day is much more enjoyable. "

to stop with military zeal and precision. It becomes a contest: how soon can I finish them? What's the world record time for completing three errands?

Clearly, this scenario is not ideal and, fortunately, there is a better way.

When I start my day by going to the gym for an hour or two or by doing a volunteer shift at the hospital, I experience wonderfully therapeutic effects that enhance the rest of my day. When I walk out of the gym or the hospital, I'm at least a little bit tired. This is a good thing, not only because it makes me healthier, but also because it leaves me better prepared for the rest of my day.

When I arrive back home after a busy, active morning, I normally have lunch, and because I have burned up so much energy already, I am better able to take my time with it and savor it. Then, when I take the dog for a walk, we linger a bit and enjoy the day, feeling lucky to be alive on such a fine day. When I do my errands, I'm not so inclined to rush through them and might even notice some interesting details along the way.

After I return home from my errands, sometimes I take a little catnap (don't tell my dog Munson I call it that!). By evening, I'm ready to settle down and read the newspaper or a magazine (actually *reading* the articles) or watch some TV. At bedtime, I fall asleep more easily.

Voila! Miraculously, I have achieved the desired effect. I have started out my day in a positive and productive way, which also burns off some energy, preparing me to keep a more even pace and feel more relaxed throughout the remainder of the day. Everyone benefits—my dog, my wife, me, and even the store clerk who gets to interact with a more patient and relaxed customer.

For these reasons, exercise and other energy-consuming activities like volunteering and part-time work are extremely valuable for Type As when they retire. They provide a useful way to expend energy and allow us to more easily pace ourselves and enjoy the simple things in life.

.

THE PROS AND CONS OF TRAVEL

> For pragmatic reasons, I love the routine.
> I know my life is kind of orderly, I just like that better.
> —Andrea Martin

Like most people, I have always enjoyed travel. Depending on where you decide to go and how you structure it, a vacation can be fast-paced or no pace at all, far-flung or closer to home, to a new destination or familiar territory. Whatever you do, it's refreshing and regenerating to leave your daily routine behind for a while.

Finally the time for travel!

The one thing I particularly disliked about corporate life was the meager amount of vacation time. Usually, I was eligible for three weeks of vacation, which is what most companies offer. Those of you who are still working and get more than this, good for you; you are very fortunate to have more time to experience life outside of work.

Three weeks of vacation usually break down something like this. You spend a week's worth of vacation throughout the winter holidays to give you more time with your family during this festive time, especially if you have children since they are off from school. This leaves you two weeks of vacation for the remaining fifty weeks of the year. You might take one weeklong trip to visit out-of-state family; hopefully, the remaining week is a real vacation, because the rest of the year is work, work, work.

Most people don't use more than one week of vacation at a time, because if they did, they would have to wait *forever* until their next vacation, the prospect of which could prove to be clinically depressing. Yet, when you take only a week at a time, here's what happens, especially with people who have Type A personalities: You rush around at work the week before your trip, trying to get things in order for when you will be gone, because you are very conscientious. As a result, you have a hard time relaxing on your first couple of vacation days. Hopefully, by day three or so, you are fully relaxed and enjoying yourself. Unfortunately, by day five, you are starting to anticipate going back to work. Projects loom before you, and you know work is accumulating on your unmanned desk or wherever you work. It is difficult to keep this picture out of your consciousness. Besides, you want to be "ready to go" when you get back, because you are a control-oriented Type A. What does this situation leave you with? Two days of truly relaxing and blissful vacation time. This is less than ideal.

I always greatly disliked and even resented the lack of time away from work. It gave me no opportunity to really relax and let go for a sustained period, let alone explore one of my hobbies in depth or try a new area of interest.

In the middle of my career, I dreamed of retiring. I used to think, "After I retire, if I have the money, you won't be able to *find me*! I'm going to be traveling all the time. You will be as likely to get a postcard from Tahiti as to have an actual Tim sighting!"

Well, as luck would have it, I was afforded the tremendous good fortune of retiring early, healthy and with discretionary funds. How many people get to do that?

My travel plans were on.

Advantages and disadvantages of travel

My wife and I traveled often in our first two years of retirement, taking several trips in the US and a couple to foreign destinations. It was interesting, fun, and sometimes relaxing. I also learned, however, that travel can be a bit stressful and taxing. Short, domestic vacations are not particularly demanding, but if you do them in succession, they can be somewhat dizzying. Returning from one trip only to turn around and head back out can be disorienting.

> " I used to think, 'After I retire, if I have the money, you won't be able to find me!' "

Foreign travel entails many additional complications. Long flights, often with a couple of connections, as well as language, currency, and cultural differences, add up to a lot of stress. Also, the sightseeing that usually accompanies such trips, while interesting, can be draining. Remember to take into account that this reaction is coming from a relatively young and healthy retiree. Since many of you will not be as fortunate in this respect, you may find foreign travel even more daunting that I do.

There is another factor when considering your travel plans in retirement. Many Type As are creatures of habit, as I am, and they may enjoy their daily routines more than they realize. For people like this, travel is enjoyable, but it can turn a little negative in too large a dose.

I am not trying to persuade you to forego travel in retirement. It is often well worth the effort and expense, and I don't at all regret my travel experiences. Also, I have some retired friends who have been traveling extensively for years and years, and they seem to love all aspects of it, or at least don't experience the downsides as acutely as I do.

Experiment to find what works for you

My view is that travel has both positive and negative aspects and, as with most pursuits in life, how you incorporate it into your retired life is a personal decision based on your particular likes and dislikes and your budget. Experiment with it, and keep an open mind, and you will find what works best for you.

Once I discovered what my passions were and developed priorities and a purpose in life, I enjoy my life much more than I did when I had a corporate job. I love my daily life now. This means I now compare travel, with its inherent tradeoffs, to a fun daily routine rather than to a work life that I often desired to escape. Yes, I still like to get away, but it is not as though I *need* to get away any more.

I have a couple of suggestions about how to enjoy international travel with less wear and tear. If you plan to visit more than one city on your trip abroad, you can reduce the stress by opting for a cruise or a relaxed-pace, land-based guided tour vacation. Cruises are much less stressful than multi-city land-based trips because, once you are settled into your stateroom, you are there for the duration of your vacation. You don't have to pack up every two days and travel by car, bus, train, or airplane to your next destination; unpack at the next hotel; and get oriented to your new locale. Also, because you are on the ship for much of the time, you have less exposure to the complications of the local culture's language, unfamiliar currency, and differing customs, such as how to dress appropriately and how much to tip at a restaurant. To be fair, the flip side is that a cruise, with short stays at each port, allows you much less time and opportunity to immerse yourself in the local culture, which is important to some travelers.

Land-based guided tour packages allow you to purchase a complete itinerary of flights, hotels, daily excursions, and all related transportation for multi-city destinations in certain regions or countries of the world. This can be a great option for retirees who want to fully engage in a different culture in a way not possible on a cruise, yet want to skip all the planning that would be necessary if you tried to schedule the trip yourself. However, I recommend land-based tours that offer a more relaxed pace. Many tour packages require you to get up very early every morning and tour for eight hours each day. Some more relaxing tours have you visit just one local attraction a day, either in the morning or afternoon, leaving the rest of the day available for you to use as you wish. You might choose to use that unscheduled time to visit a park or plaza, sip some coffee or wine at an outdoor restaurant, or just wander around the city. In the lingo of my principles of Type A retirement, this gives you the opportunity to savor the simple things and more fully enjoy the process and "open time."

Regular tours are for you if you want to see "everything" on your vacation and don't care about relaxing.

While international trips are great, most of us, me included, tend to take our homeland for granted. We may not have seen much of our home countries, which are right there in front of us and much easier and cheaper to access than are foreign countries. My wife and I created an extensive and varied list of US destinations that we plan to visit. Some of these areas are of interest because of their natural beauty, such as Hawaii and Alaska. Some have an alluring charm, such as Savannah or New England. Other destinations offer high-energy, urban-style activities, such as New York City and Las Vegas.

You probably will choose to travel in retirement, either a little or a lot. I think that's great. At the same time, I hope you also find that you love your daily life in retirement, as I have come to, and that travel is just icing on the cake.

YOUR NEW ACHIEVEMENT
PERSONAL BALANCE

> " I arise in the morning torn between a desire to improve the world and a desire to enjoy the world. This makes it hard to plan the day. "
>
> —E. B. White

BE AVAILABLE TO RESPOND TO LIFE

Since the Lord is directing our steps, why try to understand everything that happens along the way?

—Proverbs 20:24

I began the book with the observation that many Type As are anxious about the prospect of retiring. The open space of retirement is daunting, especially for driven and achievement-oriented people, or even for those Type As who just like to be busy and occupied all the time.

I have addressed the challenges of retirement for Type A personalities in two ways. First, I discussed how you can play to your strengths, that is, use your natural abilities and inclinations as a Type A to pursue your passions and find purpose in life during retirement. In your work life, you enjoyed being busy, productive, and accomplishing goals. I have shown you how in retirement you can likewise choose goals that are personally meaningful for this new stage of your life and harness your tremendous energy to pursue them. You have always thrived on having some structure in your life. Full-time retirement requires some structuring, and you have the talents and tools to create it. I have shown how you can use your inherent skills as a Type

A and the extra time you are afforded in retirement to make a positive impact on yourself, others, and the community.

The second prong of my retirement strategy for Type As, expanding yourself, has to do with expanding your comfort zone in retirement to include taking your time with and enjoying the process of your activities. You can learn to fully experience and even relish the simple things in life, such as playing with the grandchildren, going for a walk after dinner with your spouse, or preparing a meal. You can find more joy in everyday activities if you allow yourself. It is perfectly all right and in fact quite good for you to take time for yourself, pace yourself, and just plain relax. I have given you tools like Vipassana meditation that will help you develop inner calm and greater self-awareness. You can learn to savor your experiences, which will deepen your enjoyment. Increasing the time you spend engaging in pleasurable and meaningful activities, along with rest and relaxation, will help you fill the space that is created by the lack of full-time work in retirement.

The existential vacuum

I will now offer one additional perspective to ponder as you move into retirement, which was suggested by Dr. Viktor E. Frankl, a survivor of four Nazi death camps, including Auschwitz, in his seminal work, *Man's Search for Meaning*. Along with his fascinating personal story and many insights into the meaning of our existence, Frankl's book describes what he calls an "existential vacuum," which he believes pervades modern society. Frankl writes:

Man has suffered a loss in his more recent development inasmuch as the traditions which buttressed his behavior are now rapidly diminishing. No instinct tells him what he has to do, and no tradition tells him what he ought to do; sometimes he does not even know what he wishes to do ... [This] existential vacuum manifests itself in a state of boredom (p. 106).

Frankl goes on to say that, in an effort to fill this existential vacuum, we need to stop asking what the meaning of life is, because it varies from person to person. According to Frankl, it is not even useful to try to decipher our own personal meaning, since it also varies from moment to moment. (By advocating this, I'll admit that Frankl is discounting what I advocate, which is the importance of developing a purpose. Still, I recognize the value of his point.) He says that rather than struggling with the meaning of our existence, we should simply "think of ourselves as those who were being questioned by life—daily and hourly" (p. 77). By this, he means that we should just let life unfold and respond to it in a meaningful way as it presents opportunities and challenges.

Frankl states: "... it [does] not really matter what we expect from life, but rather *what life expects from us*" (p. 77, italics added). He is saying that it is best to simply make yourself "available" to

> " Frankl says that rather than struggling with the meaning of our existence, we should simply 'think of ourselves as those who were being questioned by life—daily and hourly.' "

life. He goes on to state: "Our answer must consist…in right action and right conduct. Life ultimately means taking the responsibility to find the right answer to its problems and to fulfill the tasks which it constantly sets for each individual" (p. 77).

I would modify Frankl's concept slightly; at least for me, it is not what "life" expects from me that concerns me, but rather what God expects from me.

Planning versus responding to life or God

This idea that we cannot script out our lives in any meaningful way, and rather should simply make ourselves "available" to life or God, I have found to be resoundingly true. When I was in the midst of my working life, I'd sometimes sit down and attempt to map out my future career path. I'd predict one or two transfers or promotions ahead, positions I thought I might get. It fascinates me to note how inaccurate my plans turned out to be. As an example, at one point I anticipated that my next career move would be a promotion to manager in the department I was working in, which would have been the logical move. Just a couple of days after making this prediction, I received a call from the CFO of a sister company, offering me the position of heading up a new department. It was not at all what I expected. What did I do? I simply *responded* to this unexpected development, as Frankl suggests. I learned more about the sister company, investigated the new opportunity, considered my options, and made the decision to take the new job. In Frankl's terms, I reacted to the unforeseen opportunity that presented itself with productive and "right" action. This position turned out to be a better move for me than the position I had "planned" to take. All the planning I had done earlier was of no use.

Is Frankl also correct in his assertion that a personal purpose has no value? I think he would agree that having a sense of personal priorities and direction is not wholly without worth. Making the decision that your family, your work, a cause, or some such priority is a good way to use your unique talents and interests has at least some benefit as a guide to your day-to-day actions.

> " It might be best not to fill **all** of our time with goals and structured activities so as to be more available to what life and God have to offer. "

However, Frankl's overall point is well taken. It might be best to not fill *all* of our time with goals and structured activities so as to be more available to what life and God have to offer. Who knows what interesting and useful challenges will present themselves? And do we want to already be fully occupied and "spoken for" when truly important needs arise?

Keep free time in your schedule to relax and be available

Influenced by Frankl, over the past couple of years, I have chosen not to overload my schedule with too many goals and activities. Doing so provided me with time to pace myself, relax, and enjoy open time. What is more, I was available to assist close family members with some unexpected and very difficult challenges. All of these crises occurred nearly simultaneously.

First, my dad became gravely ill with lung cancer. My brother and sister, who both still work and live farther away from Dad than I do, were unable to help as much as they would have liked due to work commitments and distance. My dad required daily care and assistance while he was still living in his condo, which I was able to provide. When he needed to move to a nursing home, I had the time to do the research and find the one that best suited his needs. Once he was in the nursing home, I sat with him every day and kept him company. Because we had such long stretches of time together, my father and I shared stories. Dad had never been one to share his feelings, but near the end of his life, he was very open with me. I learned a great deal about his childhood and his early years as a Chicago firefighter. As a young man straight out of cadet training, he was tremendously brave and fought raging fires. His stories were fascinating and endearing. Sadly, after a couple of weeks in the nursing home, he passed away.

During the time Dad was sick, my brother was going through a divorce after twenty-seven years of marriage. My schedule had enough room in it that I had plenty of time to provide him with emotional support and occasional legal advice during the difficult transition.

After our father died, my sister decided to move to another part of the country. She was moving to where my wife and I spend part of the winter each year, so I was able to assist her with choosing a neighborhood, purchasing a new home, and getting oriented to the new locale.

Whew! It was a busy year. But it was good that I had kept time to be available to my family during this tumultuous period.

Likewise, my wife also makes time to be available to our families. She has many fewer Type A characteristics than I do, so prior to retirement she had not worried as much about how she would fill her time when the time came. Being more child-oriented and patient than me, she helps a lot with the kids in our extended family. As an example, one of our young nieces had two children in the last couple of years, and she is unmarried. It's quite a struggle for her and the young ones, as you might suspect. Elaine babysits her children regularly and uses her experience as a preschool teacher to provide meaningful, educational play for the children while she is caring for them. She also takes several of our younger nieces and nephews to the movies occasionally to see an animated children's feature, or has them over to our house around the holidays to do fun things like make sugar cookies or build gingerbread houses.

We both have made the conscious effort to be available to family and friends during retirement, and we have found it very worthwhile and enjoyable. It is interesting to see what life and God have in store for us, and I believe it also makes for the best use of our time and energy. Sure, we could fill our schedules with more goals and tasks, but many of these would be just "make work." If you completely fill up your time in retirement with planned goals and tasks, you will probably miss out on, or spend little time on, the most important things. Make time available in your schedule when family and friends call for help, or often you will be too busy to provide help, and after a while, understandably, they might just stop calling.

In the same way, if you quiet your mind and make yourself available to Him, God will occasionally "call" you with a thought on how you might use your time and talents to be of service.

He too may stop calling if you are always too busy.

BALANCE IS THE KEY

> The most general law in nature is equity—
> the principle of balance and symmetry.
>
> —Herbert Read

It's a bit of a cliché, and for that I apologize, but it is also very true: life is a journey.

If you are going on any journey, you need to have a destination, right? Otherwise, you will just wander about aimlessly. That's not an ideal scenario, especially for goal-oriented people like Type As.

But would it be enough to just have a destination and eventually arrive at it? Don't you want to enjoy the journey, too? Isn't the unfolding of the experience almost as important, or maybe even more important, than getting there?

In life, and specifically your life in retirement, you can benefit from having a "destination": finding your passions, ordering your priorities, and choosing a single, compelling purpose to focus on. As well, you want to enjoy each step of the way and can do so by expanding your viewpoint to embrace joyfulness and relaxation.

I'll admit, I have provided you with what might appear to be two contradictory and mutually exclusive approaches to retirement:

- Use your God-given Type A talents to get out there and go for it all.

- Relax, slow down, and savor the simple things in life.

> " I contend that life at its very essence involves many such seeming contradictions, and we are continually challenged to find balance among them— our own, personal balance. "

However, I contend that life at its very essence involves many such seeming contradictions, and we are continually challenged to find balance among them— our own, personal balance.

For example, how do you decide how serious a person you should be or how carefree? Well, you don't want to be serious all of the time. That would be bad for your health and overall well-being, and it simply isn't necessary. On the other hand, you don't want to be a clown all day and night, either; that would be inappropriate at work or when disciplining your child or discussing finances with your spouse.

And how much should you value money? If it is all you focus on, you will miss much of what is wonderful in life, such as close family relationships, enjoyable hobbies, and relaxing downtime. Yet, if you ignore money completely, you will probably suffer more than you need to and you won't have the peace of mind that comes with having secure finances.

With most things in life, balance is the key.

This goes for retirement, too, and for how you apply the principles I have suggested. You must find and maintain a balance, one that suits you personally. If you were to spend all your time in retirement relaxing, most likely you would become mind-numbingly bored, especially since you are a Type A. Yet, if you were to focus on goals and achievement exclusively, you would miss much of the benefit of being retired, which is to kick back a little, smell the roses, and allow life to unfold before you.

Remember, too, the balance that is right for you will almost certainly change over time as situations change and as you evolve. Strive to maintain a flexible attitude to maintain your balance.

For example, at some point, you might choose to pursue a challenging project that keeps you very busy and focused for several days or weeks. That's fine; just try not to become obsessed with it, which will be harmful to your emotional balance. In fact, it is not necessary to become obsessed with most post-retirement goals, because they tend to be less than critical. When your challenging project has been completed, it might be a good idea to rest for a while and collect your thoughts rather than immediately throw yourself into another new project. It's about maintaining balance, remember? As we age, we naturally slow down a bit, anyway. Rather than deny it and fight against it, embrace these natural changes.

Being an industrious Type A, no doubt you will go through cycles during retirement, as I have—running around being an industrious Type A much of the time, and then realizing the unnecessary and sometimes harmful nature of this, and then pacing and relaxing for awhile. Cycles like this are not only to be expected, but they are probably healthy and good, too. Just remember, there are no right answers in retirement, only what feels right to you.

Good luck! However, I know you don't need it. Type As generally don't need to rely on luck!

NOTES

Visit **Type-A-Lifestyle.com**
to find interesting ideas
& tips for better living.

Living • Money • Diet & Exercise • Stress & Anxiety